Buying your FREEHOLD *or extending your* LEASE

The flat owner's
guide to
leasehold
enfranchisement

Timothy Curran

A Publication by Leasehold Enfranchisement Limited

Leasehold Enfranchisement Limited is a firm of chartered surveyors
specialising in the leasehold enfranchisement of flats

**Written by Timothy Curran for
and published in the United Kingdom by
Leasehold Enfranchisement Limited
104 Ramillies Road
London W4 1JA**

First published 1993

ISBN 0 9522232 0 1

Edited, packaged and produced by
Aldridge Press
24, Thorney Hedge Road,
London W4 5SD

Designed by Geoffrey Wadsley
Illustrations by Julia Osorno
Printed by Ian Allan Printing Ltd.
Addlestone, Surrey

Contents

Acknowledgements

Leasehold Enfranchisement Limited gratefully
acknowledges the contributions made to this book by the
following consultants:

Giles Thorman, Solicitor, Collyer-Bristow, London WC1

Chris Green, Valuer, Barnard Marcus, London W11

David North and David Mackenzie, Chartered
Accountants, Bowker Orford & Co., London W1

The views and opinions expressed in this book are the
responsibility of Leasehold Enfranchisement Limited.
While every effort has been made to ensure accuracy
throughout this book, readers are strongly advised to
obtain professional advice on their particular
circumstances.

The names of the companies, individuals and properties
in the examples are fictitious unless stated otherwise, and
any coincidences with or similarities to actual companies,
individuals or properties are unintended.

Useful addresses

The Royal Institution
of Chartered Surveyors
12, Great George Street
London SW1P 3AD
Tel: 071 222 7000

HM Inspector of Taxes
Public Enquiry Unit
Somerset House
London WC2R 1LB
Tel: 071 438 6420

The Incorporated Society
of Valuers and Auctioneers
3, Cadogan Gate
London SW1X 0AS
Tel: 071 235 2282

The Council of Mortgage
Lenders
3, Savile Row
London W1X 1AF
Tel: 071 437 0655

The Law Society
113 Chancery Lane
London WC2A 1PL
Tel: 071 242 1222

CHAPTER 1

Introduction

"Leasehold as a form of tenure is deeply unsatisfactory."

This comment by the Housing Minister, Sir George Young, on BBC's Question Time in February 1993 echoes, and probably understates, the views of many flat owners.

The litany of complaints by flat owners in recent years is a familiar story of high service charges, problems with repairs and difficulties in contacting the freeholder.

A minority do have responsible freeholders who manage their buildings effectively. Many flat owners, however, suffer from persistent problems caused by the freeholder's action or inaction. Others find that their freeholder provides an indifferent or ineffective service, or is unwilling to renew their lease on reasonable terms. Sometimes it is not the freeholder who is the problem but the landlord who owns the head lease.

YOUR NEW RIGHTS AND THIS GUIDE

The Leasehold Reform, Housing and Urban Development Act, 1993, (the Act) creates new rights for most flat owners in England and Wales. These new rights of leasehold enfranchisement are:

- To collectively purchase the freehold, known as 'collective enfranchisement'
- To extend your lease.

According to the 1991 census there were approximately 1.1 million owner-occupied flats in England and Wales. Only a small proportion of these flat owners own their freeholds already or have extended their leases. Hundreds of thousands of flat owners could benefit from the new rights.

It remains to be seen how the Act will change the flat market but there is no doubt it will change. Owners will want to know if they can collectively enfranchise or extend their leases and how this will affect values. Buyers will ask whether the new rights apply and will want to take this into account in the price they pay. The market for shorter leases should improve. Freeholders will have to decide whether to sell voluntarily before flat owners claim their new rights.

ABOUT THIS GUIDE

This guide has been written to provide you, the flat owner, with a step by step guide to your new rights. It will answer these questions:

- What does collective enfranchisement or a lease extension mean?
- Who is eligible?
- What will it save and cost? Is it worth it?
- What do I, and my fellow flat owners, have to do?
- Who actually owns the freehold after collective enfranchisement and how should we manage it?
- How can I raise the money?
- What are the tax implications of collective enfranchisement and lease extensions?

The aim of this guide is to provide clear, practical answers to these questions, to explain the issues and to point out their implications. This will help you to understand the financial, legal and property management aspects and to ask your solicitor and surveyor the relevant questions for your circumstances. The result should be to give you more control over the cost and direction of your collective enfranchisement or lease extension.

This guide deals only with the law in England and Wales and does not:

- Replace the need for professional advice on your own position
- Provide answers to detailed questions about particular circumstances
- Give advice on the leasehold enfranchisement of houses – as distinct from flats.

It is inevitable that the full interpretation of the new rights and procedures in the Act will take some time to settle down. It will be affected by subsequent Government regulations, leasehold valuation tribunal and court decisions and accepted practice. The new rights do not apply in Scotland and Northern Ireland.

How to use this guide

Chapter 2 examines who is eligible for collective enfranchisement and lease extensions. Chapter 3 explains the potential savings, benefits and costs, describes how to estimate them and helps you decide whether collective enfranchisement or a lease extension are worthwhile.

Chapters 4, 6, 7 and 8 deal with converting your rights of collective enfranchisement into practice and the implications of owning and managing the freehold. Chapters 5 and 7 deal with the practical aspects of claiming a lease extension, and if you need it, raising a mortgage or loan.

Throughout the guide you will see four special features which have been designed to emphasise a particular issue or to summarise key points in the text. These are:

TAKE CARE !

This warns you of potentially costly or difficult situations, which may occur.

This device is used to highlight where you will need to take professional advice, for example, from a valuer or a solicitor.

TIP

To suggest solutions to potential problems you might face in collectively purchasing your freehold or extending your lease.

Checklists used to summarise key points, such as:

The new rights check
• Collective enfranchisement
• Lease extension

Technical terms

Legal and technical terms have been avoided where this is possible. The terms which have been used are explained in the glossary at the end of the book.

THE BACKGROUND: FREEHOLD AND LEASEHOLD

Under English law a block of flats or a house converted into flats can have a fragmented ownership. Various people can simultaneously own different interests in the same property. The differences concern the length of the ownership, the amount of property owned and the conditions under which the property is owned.

Owning the freehold interest means, in effect, that you own it forever. On the other hand you own a leasehold interest for a fixed period. The conditions of ownership, or 'tenure', are usually more extensive for leasehold than freehold ownership. This is why some people avoid leasehold flats, choosing a freehold house instead.

The freehold interest in a block of flats, or a house converted into flats, is separate from the leasehold interests of the flat owners, even when the flat owners also own the freehold. An added complication is that the freeholder sometimes creates a leasehold interest of the whole building, such as a head lease. The Act refers to this as an intermediate leasehold interest.

The flat owners' leases set out the conditions under which the property is held and describe the responsibilities for repairs and management. This structure of interests for the freeholder, intermediate leaseholder and flat owners is shown in the diagram opposite.

Is leasehold tenure deeply unsatisfactory?

Our system of leasehold tenure has evolved over hundreds of years. It is in many situations a flexible, well designed and mutually satisfactory way of owning property for both landlord and tenant. Owner-occupied leasehold flats are the exception – the cul-de-sac in the otherwise successful evolution of leasehold tenure.

The root of the problem is that the freeholder, or the intermediate leaseholder, is almost always responsible for the repair, insurance and management of the building. This happens despite the fact that usually they have the minority financial investment in the building. The flat owners can influence but ultimately cannot control the freeholder or intermediate leaseholder. This too is despite the fact that, in most situations, they have the majority financial investment.

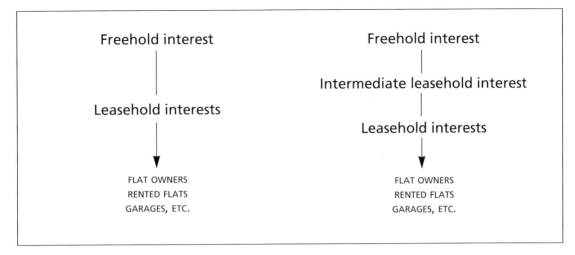

Freehold interest   Freehold interest

Leasehold interests   Intermediate leasehold interest

                          Leasehold interests

FLAT OWNERS   FLAT OWNERS
RENTED FLATS   RENTED FLATS
GARAGES, ETC.   GARAGES, ETC.

Freehold and leasehold interests

Wasting asset

Until the Act was passed an allied problem was that, after a time, most leases declined in value without flat owners having the statutory right to extend their leases. In some situations their leases became what are known as 'wasting assets'.

The problem might not have been apparent at first but it certainly became so in the long term. As the years went by a valuable long lease degenerated into a less valuable short lease which became more difficult to sell. The Act's new rights to a lease extension mean that most flat owners can now overcome the problems of declining lease values.

Owner-occupation

Owner-occupied flats are a relatively new phenomenon as, previously, most people who lived in flats rented them. The increase in owner-occupied flats over the last few decades has been made possible by the leasehold tenure system being adapted to a type of owner-occupation for which it was never designed.

The consequent problems have resulted in a series of moves to strengthen the rights of flat owners against their landlords. The new rights of leasehold enfranchisement are part of this continuing story. It is worth noting that many lessees of houses were given rights of leasehold enfranchisement a quarter of a century ago.

Freehold ownership

Given the problems and complications of leasehold ownership, you may wonder why flats are not sold on a freehold basis, without any leasehold interests involved. The position in Scotland is similar to this. Each flat owner usually owns a share in the common structure and common parts and contributes to their upkeep.

In England and Wales the situation is different. By a quirk of the law it can be difficult, sometimes impossible, to enforce a flat owner's positive obligations when a flat is owned on a freehold basis. These positive obligations, which are also called covenants, include the obligations to repair or to pay a service charge.

The result of this problem in enforcing freehold positive obligations is that all flat owners in a building can suffer. As a consequence freehold flats are relatively rare, and can be difficult to sell or mortgage.

It has also been in the freeholder's financial interest to sell flats on a leasehold basis, especially when the flat was sold on a relatively short lease. Before the Act was passed the freeholder could look forward to the prospect of negotiating a lease renewal from a position of strength since the flat owner had no right to the renewal.

British Governments have considered changing the law to overcome this anomaly. So far there has been much discussion and a few reports, but no action. Other countries which inherited a leasehold system, such as Australia and Canada, have adopted forms of co-ownership for flats. The British Government is considering a form of co-ownership for flats, discussed later on in this chapter, called 'commonhold'.

Enforcement problems

Flat owners' positive obligations, or covenants, can be enforced where they own their flats on a leasehold basis. The legal structure of a freeholder owning the building, with the flats being held on a leasehold basis, allows the rights and obligations of the freeholder and leaseholders to be enforced, at least in theory.

In practice, there can be problems in enforcing these rights and obligations. Freeholders can fail to carry out repairs or otherwise mismanage the property. Leaseholders sometimes refuse to pay or delay paying their service charges, which can leave the freeholder without the money to carry out the repairs. A cycle of mistrust and recrimination can set in.

One solution is for the leasehold flat owners to acquire the freehold. This does not change their leasehold flats into freehold flats but, as owners of the freehold, they can repair and manage the property in line with their own wishes. They can also grant longer leases.

Even where the relationship of freeholder and lease-holder is harmonious, there is the problem of the lease declining in value. The two ways to overcome this problem are by extending the lease or acquiring the freehold.

WHAT ARE YOUR NEW RIGHTS?

This section provides an overview of leaseholders' new rights.

Collective enfranchisement

Collective enfranchisement is the right, provided certain conditions are met, for flat owners to collectively purchase their freehold. This right to purchase also applies to inter-mediate leasehold interests. The freeholder and any intermediate landlords have to sell.

What does collective enfranchisement mean in practice?
The example below shows what could happen.

EXAMPLE

Collective enfranchisement of Elgar House
Elgar House is an Edwardian block of 25 flats. Twenty-three of the flats are owned on long leases, each having 55 years to run. The remaining two flats are rented out on a monthly basis. The block has a small newspaper and tobacconist kiosk at its front entrance, a communal garden, and at its rear boundary there is a row of garages which are leased to the flat owners. The basement store rooms are also leased to the flat owners.

At the turn of this century the freeholder, Perpetual Estates Limited, granted a 150 year lease of the whole block to a family trust. This intermediate leasehold interest has now been acquired by Ransom Investments Limited, which is the landlord to the 25 flats, the kiosk, store rooms and the garages. Ransom Investments Limited is responsible under its lease from Perpetual Estates Limited for repairing and managing the block.

True to its name, Ransom Investments Limited seems more interested in increasing the service charges than mending the roof properly. It will not even consider granting longer leases to the flat owners who find that their relatively short leases are increasingly difficult to sell.

However, the building and the flat owners are eligible for collective enfranchisement. Twenty of the 23 flat owners decide to collectively enfranchise. They form a company, Elgar House Limited, and exercise their right under the Act to acquire the freehold from Perpetual Estates Limited and the intermediate leasehold from Ransom Investments Limited.

The situation after collective enfranchisement is that:

○ Elgar House Limited owns the freehold and the intermediate leasehold interest.

○ Elgar House Limited becomes the landlord for all the 25 flats, the kiosk, the store rooms and the garages.

○ The 20 flat owners who are shareholders in Elgar House Limited control the maintenance and management of the block.

○ The change of ownership of the freehold and intermediate leasehold does not in itself affect any of the flat owners' existing leases.

○ Elgar House Limited can now grant longer leases, or with consent of the tenants, can vary existing leases.

Comment

In this example Elgar House Limited is what the Act refers to as the nominee purchaser. The company as nominee purchaser acts as the buyer on behalf of all the participating flat owners and negotiates with the freeholder and the intermediate leaseholder.

Lease extension

Flat owners who meet certain conditions are eligible, as individuals, for lease extensions. The new, extended lease is granted for 90 years plus the remaining period of the old lease. The ground rent is reduced to a peppercorn rent (which means no rent is paid) and, with a few exceptions, the new lease's terms are the same as the old lease.

What does a lease extension mean in practice?

The example below demonstrates what could happen.

EXAMPLE

Mrs Williams extends her lease

Merlin Court is a block of twelve flats situated over a parade of shops. Thirty-three years ago the freeholder, Mooncrest Dairies Limited, sold five of the flats on 90 year leases. The remaining seven flats are rented out on a monthly basis.

One of the flat owners, Mrs Williams, wants to sell her flat so she can retire to the country.

Unfortunately, her lease only has 57 years left which makes it difficult to sell since most flats in the area have longer leases. Her ground rent is £50 per year and she pays a fixed service charge, established when the lease was granted, of £25 per year. Mooncrest Dairies Limited appear more interested in expanding into home delivered videos than dealing with Mrs Williams' letters requesting a lease extension.

Mrs Williams investigates her new rights under the Act, finding that Merlin Court does not qualify for collective enfranchisement because the area of the shops exceeds 10% of the residential area. She is eligible for a lease extension and claims her new right.

What happens subsequently is that:

○ Mrs Williams obtains a new 147 year lease from the landlord, Mooncrest Dairies Limited, based on the 57 years left on her old lease plus a further 90 years.

○ Her ground rent is reduced to a peppercorn.

○ The terms of her new lease include a variable service charge but, apart from the ground rent, are essentially the same as before.

○ The freeholder/leaseholder relationship remains the same, apart from the length, rent and new service charge provision of the lease. Mrs Williams' new lease does not give her any more control over her landlord.

Comment

The situation would have been more complicated if Mooncrest Dairies Limited had granted an intermediate leasehold interest of the shops and flats, perhaps to Ransom Investments Limited. In that situation Ransom Investments Limited would have granted the extended lease, provided its own lease was long enough. In Mrs Williams' case, Ransom Investments Limited would have needed at least 147 years left on its lease.

Will it be too expensive and complicated to claim the new rights?

The short answer in most cases is 'No'.

There is no reason why collective enfranchisement in a block of, say, twelve flats, or in a house converted into flats, should be too complicated or, if the leases are reasonably long, too expensive. It could be more complicated and more expensive in some larger blocks of flats, especially when the leases are relatively short.

In the medium to longer term the cost of not owning your freehold could prove to be more expensive and the associated problems more time consuming.

It should be reasonably straightforward to claim a lease extension. While the cost will depend largely on the length of your existing lease, the result will be a more valuable, and saleable, asset. At least you will not have to rely on your landlord's rather unreliable and potentially expensive goodwill to obtain the lease extension.

Many potential claims for collective enfranchisement and lease extensions may in practice end up as negotiated sales of the freehold or as negotiated lease extensions outside the framework of the Act. However, this depends on whether all parties involved prefer to avoid the statutory route.

The Act will affect the investment market for residential freeholds, especially where flat owners have extended their leases and the freeholder does not have any ground rent income. This means that, increasingly, freeholders may offer to sell their freeholds to flat owners in their properties.

People and property

The wise old men of the property profession say that property is mainly about people. This is a view shared by the wiser of their colleagues, regardless of sex or age. Property professionals stumble at the first hurdle when they forget this elementary truth.

Leasehold enfranchisement is primarily about your rights to your home. But putting your rights into practice means dealing with people. It involves negotiations with the freeholder or landlord, possibly where there has been a history of fraught discussions, even acrimony. This situation can produce strongly held views on both sides.

Leasehold enfranchisement also means another encounter with the property profession. No doubt your solicitor and surveyor put up a splendid performance, for modest fees, when you purchased your flat. Or were there a few problems along the way?

Collective enfranchisement brings the challenges, and rewards, of working with a group of people for a common objective. After the purchase comes the task of managing the property. This, too, involves managing people.

Returning to the example of Elgar House on page 7, how will Elgar House Limited cope with their new management responsibilities? Will the directors manage the property efficiently, administer their company Elgar House Limited properly and find time to listen responsively to their fellow shareholders and flat owners? Or will they be voted out at the next annual general meeting?

This guide is not concerned just with the technical issues in leasehold enfranchisement. It describes how flat owners, and their professional advisers, should deal with the legal, valuation and property management issues without losing sight of the needs of the individuals and groups involved. Your communication and administration skills will be crucial to your success in collective enfranchisement.

Commonhold

The new rights of leasehold enfranchisement are different from the Government's proposals for commonhold.

If these proposals become law, they would give flat owners the freehold interest in their flats. The freehold interest in the common structure and common parts of the building would belong to, and be managed by, a 'commonhold association' to which all flat owners who owned the freehold interests in their flats would belong.

There are two important points you should be aware of:

○ The commonhold proposals currently do not contain powers to compel freeholders and intermediate lease-holders to sell in order that a commonhold can be established. If you wanted to set up a commonhold, but could not agree a voluntary sale, you would have to use the collective enfranchisement route to acquire the freehold and other interests.

○ All flat owners with leases of 21 years or more would have to agree to the commonhold being formed.

> **TAKE CARE !**
>
> The commonhold proposals do not give flat owners the power to make their freeholders and intermediate leaseholders sell.

Eligibility for Leasehold Enfranchisement

If you own a flat you will want to know whether you are eligible for the new rights. The Act has enough 'ifs' and 'buts' to make this quite a complicated business. The tests described here provide the means to diagnose your prospects.

This chapter deals with:
- Eligibility for collective enfranchisement and lease extensions
- The property acquired in collective enfranchisement and the terms of the extended lease
- Choosing between collective enfranchisement and a lease extension
- Hints and tactics

INTRODUCTION

The new rights mean you can be:
○ Eligible for collective enfranchisement
  or
○ Eligible for a lease extension
  or
○ Eligible for both these rights
  or
○ In a minority of cases not eligible for either right.

Your eligibility depends on your lease, the building (referred to in the Act as the 'premises') where your flat is situated and your circumstances, such as how many other flat owners in the building want to join in the collective enfranchisement. You can take advantage of your right to a lease extension as an individual. The right to collective enfranchisement, however, can only be taken up if two or more flat owners are involved. References in this chapter to 'your eligibility' for collective enfranchisement should be understood in the context of your eligibility to participate with other flat owners.

Unfortunately, the Act's rules for eligibility are complex. This chapter helps you assess your eligibility by explaining these rules in terms of tests you have to pass. It should be emphasised that the Act was designed to give flat owners new rights, not to raise their expectations and then dash them. Most flat owners will be eligible for a lease extension, while many others will be able to choose between a lease extension and collective enfranchisement.

The key points on eligibility for collective enfranchisement and lease extensions are relatively straightforward. One point applies to both rights, which is that you must be a 'qualifying tenant'.

Collective enfranchisement ... key points on eligibility
- You must be a qualifying tenant.
- The premises where your flat is situated must pass certain tests.
- Three tests must be passed before the initial notice claiming the right to collective enfranchisement can be served.

Lease extension ... key points on eligibility
- You must be a qualifying tenant.
- You must pass the residence test.

This chapter investigates first what it is to be a qualifying tenant and then examines your eligibility for collective enfranchisement or a lease extension.

ELIGIBILITY FOR COLLECTIVE ENFRANCHISEMENT AND A LEASE EXTENSION: THE QUALIFYING TENANT

Are you a qualifying tenant?

Your lease must have four characteristics for you to be a qualifying tenant. It must be the lease of a flat, it must be a long lease, it must have a low ground rent, and it must not be one of the excluded leases. If your lease fails any one of these tests you cannot be a qualifying tenant.

Qualifying tenant check
- Lease of a flat
- Long lease
- Low ground rent
- Not an excluded lease

Do you have a lease of a flat?

In most situations it will be obvious whether you live in a flat, as opposed to a house. The Act defines a flat as a separate set of premises which fulfils all the following specifications:

○ Forms part of a building
○ Is constructed or adapted for use as a dwelling
○ The whole or a material part of the flat lies above or below some other part of the building.

The last point is particularly important since it could exclude some properties from being flats.

A building can be divided into only two flats, such as maisonettes and, since there are no restrictions on the size of the flats, it can contain flats ranging from large penthouse suites to one-room studios.

There will be some borderline cases where it will not be clear if you live in a flat. If in doubt, ask your solicitor.

Do you have a long lease ?

The principal way in which your lease can be a long lease is that it was granted for a period of 21 years or more. This means that a lease granted 45 years ago for a 60 year term is still a long lease, despite only having 15 years to run. You should check your lease to see the length, or 'term', for which it was granted.

Many flat owners do have long leases. A survey by the Consumers' Association in 1991 found that two thirds of flat owners' leases had more than 90 years to run. (This survey concentrated on converted as opposed to purpose-built properties. There is no reason to suppose the overall position is markedly different for purpose-built properties.) The situation does vary throughout England and Wales, with some long leases in central London having 60 years or considerably less to expiry.

The Act's definition of long leases covers those granted under the right to buy or rent to mortgage schemes in the Housing Act, 1985, and shared ownership leases where the tenant's share is 100%. A few rather unusual leases, such as those which are perpetually renewable or terminable after marriage or death, are included in the definition. Have a word with your solicitor if your lease appears to be excluded or is an unusual one.

Long lease definition check
• Granted for 21 years or more
• Right to buy or rent to mortgage lease
• 100% shared ownership lease
• Other specialised leases

Do you have a low ground rent?

The purpose of this test is to exclude those who rent, for instance on a monthly basis, as opposed to those who own their flats but pay a ground rent. Most flat owners' ground rents will pass the low rent test. The Consumers' Association research found that five sixths of flat owners paid ground rents of less than £100 per year. There are some landlords, again mainly in central London, who have granted long leases at ground rents which do not pass the low rent tests.

The Act's definition of low rent varies according to when the lease was granted. Understanding the Act's complex rules fully is a minority sport which you might prefer to leave to your professional advisers. In summary, the rent is a low rent if either no rent was payable in the first year or, if rent was payable, the total amount payable in the first year did not exceed:

○ For leases granted before 1/4/63, two thirds or less of the letting value of the flat when the lease commenced. Letting value here means the same as in the Leasehold Reform Act, 1967.

○ For leases granted after 31/3/63 but before 1/4/90, two thirds of the rateable value of the flat when the lease commenced.

○ For leases granted after the 31/3/90, £1,000 in Greater London, or £250 elsewhere.

> You should take professional advice on the letting value of your flat for leases granted before 1 April 1963.

You can establish if your ground rent is a low rent by finding out when your lease was granted. You can obtain the rateable value from the local authority to calculate whether your ground rent qualifies.

Rent is used here to refer to the net rent. Any insurance, service charge or other payments paid as rent should be disregarded.

Low rent definition check
- No rent in first year
- Lease granted prior to 1/4/63, take advice
- Lease granted after 31/3/63 but before 1/4/90, not exceeding two thirds of rateable value
- Lease granted after 31/3/90, not exceeding £1,000 in Greater London and £250 elsewhere
- Rent is net rent

Is your lease excluded by the Act?

The Act excludes some flat owners who have long leases at

low rents from being qualifying tenants. The main exclusions are business leases granted under the Landlord and Tenant Act, 1954. Examples of these would be the shop leases in a parade of shops which had flats on the upper floors. Other excluded leases are:

○ Where the immediate landlord is a charitable housing trust and the flat is provided by the trust as part of its charitable activity.

○ Where the landlord is the Crown. If the Crown is your landlord you are, strictly speaking, excluded from the rights of collective enfranchisement and lease extension. However the Crown has undertaken on a voluntary basis to abide by the Act's provisions in most cases. Collective enfranchisement will be refused by the Crown in certain circumstances, such as when the property has particular historical associations or where it is within a Royal Park, or adjacent to Regents Park. The Crown will be prepared to negotiate new leases in these circumstances.

○ Some leases granted contrary to the terms of a superior lease.

TIP

Although Crown leases are exempt from the Act, the Crown has undertaken to follow the Act's provisions in most cases.

Excluded leases check
• Business leases
• Some charitable housing trust leases
• Crown leases, although the Crown will abide by the Act voluntarily, with some exceptions
• Some leases granted against the terms of a superior lease

Related points about qualifying tenants

Your eligibility to be a qualifying tenant can be affected in the following ways.

Can there be more than one qualifying tenant in a flat?
If a flat is let on two long leases, both at low rents, the qualifying tenant is the tenant whose lease is inferior, in the sense of being the lowest down the chain of leases. On the other hand, if a flat is owned by joint tenants, the tenants are held jointly to be the qualifying tenant. Otherwise there is only one qualifying tenant for each flat.

EXAMPLE

Deciding who is the qualifying tenant
Perpetual Estates Limited grants Ransom Investments Limited a 99 year lease at a low rent of a flat in one of its mansion blocks. Ransom Investments then grants a 75 year

lease of the same flat, at a low rent, to Mrs Vaughan. The qualifying tenant is Mrs Vaughan.

Can you be the qualifying tenant of more than one flat?

The rule in collective enfranchisement is that if you are the qualifying tenant of more than two flats in the same premises you are excluded from being the qualifying tenant of any flat in the premises. If a company is the qualifying tenant the same rule applies for flats let to its associated companies. The purpose is to prevent one person, or a company, from exercising a disproportionate influence over the two thirds vote of qualifying tenants needed for collective enfranchisement.

The rule for a lease extension is different, for here you can be the qualifying tenant of more than two flats.

Are there restrictions about a company being a qualifying tenant?

A company can be a qualifying tenant, provided its lease is not a business lease, and it satisfies the rule above on the number of flats a qualifying tenant can have.

Do you have to occupy the flat to be a qualifying tenant?

You do not have to actually occupy the flat at the time when you participate in a claim for collective enfranchisement, or when you make your claim for a lease extension. However, both collective enfranchisement and lease extensions do have some residence requirements, which are explained on pages 24 and 28.

You can satisfy the Act's rules on occupancy by occupying only part of a flat (for instance while renting out the remainder) or by having occupied the same flat for part of the time under a different lease. In the latter situation, you could have rented the flat before you purchased it. The residence requirement can be satisfied by one tenant only where there is a joint tenancy.

Companies or other artificial persons (such as Health Authorities) cannot meet the residence requirement, because they cannot have 'homes'. The consequences are:
○ Companies cannot be included among the qualifying tenants who satisfy the collective enfranchisement residence requirement.
○ Companies and other artificial persons cannot be eligible for lease extensions.

TIP

Time spent as a sitting tenant before you purchased the same flat can be used for meeting the residence requirement.

TAKE CARE !

The existence of company-owned flats in your building may complicate your eligibility for collective enfranchisement.

Occupation check
- Only one qualifying tenant per flat
- Qualifying tenant of more than two flats is ineligible for collective enfranchisement
- Qualifying tenant of more than two flats can be eligible for lease extension
- Companies can be qualifying tenants but cannot satisfy the residence requirements
- Qualifying tenant need not occupy at time of claim

ELIGIBILITY FOR COLLECTIVE ENFRANCHISEMENT: YOUR PREMISES AND THE INITIAL NOTICE

The preceding section explained the tests for assessing whether you are a qualifying tenant. This section examines the other two key points for collective enfranchisement. Do your premises qualify and can you serve the initial notice?

Do your premises qualify?

Although the premises containing your flat must pass all the nine tests to qualify, this may not be as difficult in practice as it can seem at first. The tests are:

○ Are your premises self-contained?
○ Is the freehold of the whole building or the part of the building owned by the same person?
○ Are at least two flats in your premises held by qualifying tenants?
○ Are two thirds of the total flats held by qualifying tenants?
○ If there is a resident landlord, and if your premises are not purpose-built, do they have five or more flats?
○ Is the non-residential part within the 10% floor area limit?
○ Are your premises outside the Inheritance Tax Act designation?
○ Are your premises outside a cathedral boundary?
○ Are your premises outside the ownership of the National Trust?

The word 'premises' requires an explanation. It usually means the same as 'building'. If you live in a detached house divided into flats, or in a detached block of flats, the premises and the building which contains your flat are the same. Only in a minority, but a substantial minority, of cases will the premises and the building be different. The difference is that the premises containing your flat can be part of a larger building, as with flats in premises situated over a parade of shops.

Are your premises self-contained?
There are two ways in which your premises can be self-contained. The first is to be a structurally detached building, such as a single purpose-built block of flats as shown opposite or the detached house converted into flats mentioned above. The second is to be a self-contained part of a building which complies with the Act's rules on self-containment.

An example of a self-contained part of a building is the semi-detached house converted into flats shown opposite. The premises containing the flats in that semi-detached house are a self-contained part of a building which comply with the Act's three rules. The rules are that the self-contained part:

○ Must be divided vertically from the rest of the building, and

○ Must be capable of being redeveloped independently, and

○ Must have services which are or can be provided independently.

There will be situations where the premises are divided vertically, and could be redeveloped independently, but where the services are not provided independently. These premises could comply with the Act's rules if services could be provided to it independently of the rest of the building, but without requiring works which would cause significant interruption to the provision of services to the remainder of the building. In some situations you may need to consult a surveyor, or an engineer, to establish if the Act's rules on self-containment for the part are met, or could be achieved.

Taking a different example, the penthouse flats in the office block shown opposite are not self-contained, because they are divided horizontally – not vertically – from the rest of the building. Other examples, illustrated opposite, of premises which could be and probably would be self-contained parts of buildings are:

○ A house converted into flats in a row of terrace houses

○ A block of flats in a row of mansion block flats

○ A block of flats forming part of, but vertically separate from, the offices in an office development.

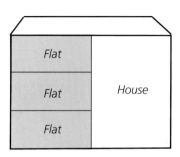

Semi-detached house converted
into flats. Self-contained premises

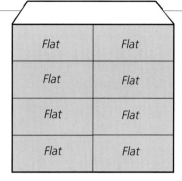

Single purpose-built block of flats
Self-contained premises

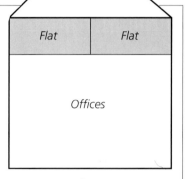

Penthouse flats. Flats are
not self-contained
part of a building

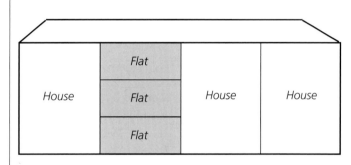

House converted into flats in a row of
terrace houses. Flats could be
self-contained part of a building

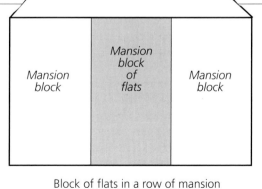

Block of flats in a row of mansion
block flats. Flats could be
self-contained part of a building

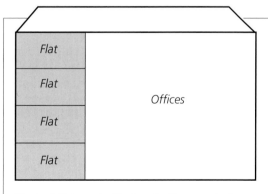

Block of flats part of but vertically separate from
offices in an office development. Flats could be
self-contained part of a building

Are your premises self-contained?

Whether or not they are self-contained depends in each case if they comply with the three rules above.

Premises self-containment check
• Structurally detached, or
• Self-contained part of a building

Is the freehold of the whole building or the part of the building owned by the same person?

The Act says that the freehold of the whole building or that part of the building must be owned by the same person. That part of the building refers to the part where your premises are.

Do your premises have at least two flats held by qualifying tenants?

You may be able to find this out by asking your neighbours, but bear in mind the point on page 18 about the ban on being the qualifying tenant of more than two flats in the premises. The Act's preliminary inquiries procedure, described on page 65, provides you with a way to find out how many qualifying tenants there are.

Are two thirds of the total flats held by qualifying tenants?

Again, you may be able to find this out from your neighbours. If not, you can obtain the answer from the preliminary inquiries.

If there is a resident landlord, and if your premises are not purpose-built, do they have five or more flats?

Part of the rationale behind this test is to protect freeholders who converted their house into flats which they sold, except for one which they retained for their own use. If your premises are purpose-built, this test does not apply.

Premises which are not purpose-built, have four or fewer flats and have a 'resident landlord' are not eligible for collective enfranchisement. Converted houses with a resident landlord but which have five or more flats will pass this test. Resident landlord here means the freeholder, not an intermediate landlord such as Ransom Investments Limited in the example on page 7. The Act's definition of resident landlord stretches to the freeholder's spouse, parent, children over eighteen and in-laws. The resident landlord must satisfy a residence test, normally but not always a year, before the exclusion operates. If you have a resident landlord you should consult your solicitor about the interpretation of the complicated residence rules.

An example of premises excluded by this test would be a converted house, divided into four flats, where the freeholder's 22 year-old son had occupied a flat for the last two years.

Resident landlord exclusion check
- Applies if not purpose-built and four or fewer flats
- Resident landlord includes spouse and child over 18
- Normally a year's residence required but complicated rules

Is the non-residential part of your premises within the 10% floor area limit?

This is one of the most controversial aspects of the Act. It makes a substantial number of flat owners who live above shops or offices ineligible for collective enfranchisement. The Act's rule is that when:

○ Part of the premises are occupied, or if vacant are intended to be occupied for non-residential purposes and

○ The internal floor area of that part or parts exceeds 10% of the internal floor area of the premises as a whole, then the premises are not eligible for collective enfranchisement. In calculating the internal floor area the common parts are disregarded completely. Garages, storage areas and similar parts used with the flats, but not included in the common areas, are treated as being residential for measurement purposes.

> It is important that the measurement complies with accepted standards of practice, so you should take professional advice on the measurement and calculation.

Collective enfranchisement which does include commercial or other non-residential parts within the 10% limit could prove to be expensive. A couple of suburban shops rented out at £6,500 each per year might be worth about £120,000 for the pair on a freehold basis. Even if they were a good investment, it could be difficult to borrow all the money. Your freeholder or another investor might be willing to lease them back, which would ease the financial burden, but you would not be able to compel your freeholder to do this.

TIP

If you are acquiring commercial property in collective enfranchisement you might be able to lease it back to the freeholder, or sell it on, reducing the capital required. Discuss this with your surveyor.

Are your premises, or other property you are seeking to buy with the premises, outside the Inheritance Tax Act designation?

Land or buildings which have been designated as of outstanding scenic, historic, architectural or scientific interest under the Inheritance Tax Act, 1984, cannot be collectively enfranchised. The preliminary inquiries procedure referred to above, allows you to find out if you are affected. Only a small minority will be caught by this test. Some flats in 'stately' homes may be affected.

Are your premises outside a cathedral boundary?

If you think you are close enough to the cathedral bells to be affected, ask your solicitor to dust down a copy of the Care of Cathedrals Measure Act, 1990, and advise. If you are inside the boundary, this will make you ineligible for collective enfranchisement.

Are your premises outside the ownership of the National Trust?

You could be excluded in certain cases if your premises are owned by the National Trust, so contact your solicitor.

> *Qualifying premises check*
> • Premises self-contained?
> • Is the freehold owned by the same person?
> • At least two flats held by qualifying tenants?
> • Are two thirds of the total flats held by qualifying tenants?
> • If resident landlord and premises not purpose-built are there five or more flats?
> • Residential part within the 10% floor area limit? Premises outside the Inheritance Tax Act designation?
> • Premises outside a cathedral boundary or ownership of the National Trust?

Can you serve the initial notice?

Qualifying tenants in eligible premises claim their right to collective enfranchisement by serving the initial notice. The qualifying tenants who serve the initial notice are known as the participating tenants. This notice can be served only when the qualifying tenants pass three tests.

○ The notice must be given by at least two thirds of the qualifying tenants in the premises.

○ The qualifying tenants who give the notice must own at least half of all the flats in the premises.

○ At least half of the qualifying tenants who give the notice must satisfy the residence requirement. The requirement is for the qualifying tenant to have occupied the flat as his or her only or principal home for the last twelve months, or for periods amounting to three years in the last ten years. It does not matter whether the qualifying tenant has used it also for other purposes.

TIP

Although companies cannot satisfy the residence requirement they can be qualifying tenants.

The Act does not allow you to participate in the initial notice when:

○ You have given a notice terminating your lease
○ Your landlord has given certain specified notices terminating your lease
○ You have to give up your flat because of a possession order
○ There are court proceedings for re-entry or forfeiture of your flat, unless the court gives you permission to participate in the initial notice
○ A compulsory purchase order has been made on your premises.

You can as an individual participate in the initial notice without being committed to taking part subsequently in the actual purchase. The other participating tenants can purchase the freehold and other interests even if one or more of the original participating tenants does not want to take part. However, in advance of serving the initial notice, you should clarify with the other participating tenants what portion of the costs you would be liable for should you not take part in the purchase.

The participating tenants as a body may withdraw the initial notice but if they do they will be liable to the reversioner, who normally is the freeholder, and other relevant landlords, for their reasonable costs up to the time of withdrawal. This is discussed further in chapter 4, page 69. It is essential that all the participating tenants understand and agree how the costs are to be apportioned between themselves if the initial notice is withdrawn, or if one of the participating tenants does not take part in the actual purchase.

You can transfer your right to participate in the collective enfranchisement to the purchaser of your flat if you sell while the claim is being negotiated. This is explained in chapter 4, page 66.

The process of working out which qualifying tenants can or should participate in the initial notice can be quite complicated, especially when there are a large number of qualifying tenants. The following example describes what could happen.

> Contact your solicitor if it seems you are prevented by the Act from participating in the initial notice, or if there is a dispute with your freeholder.

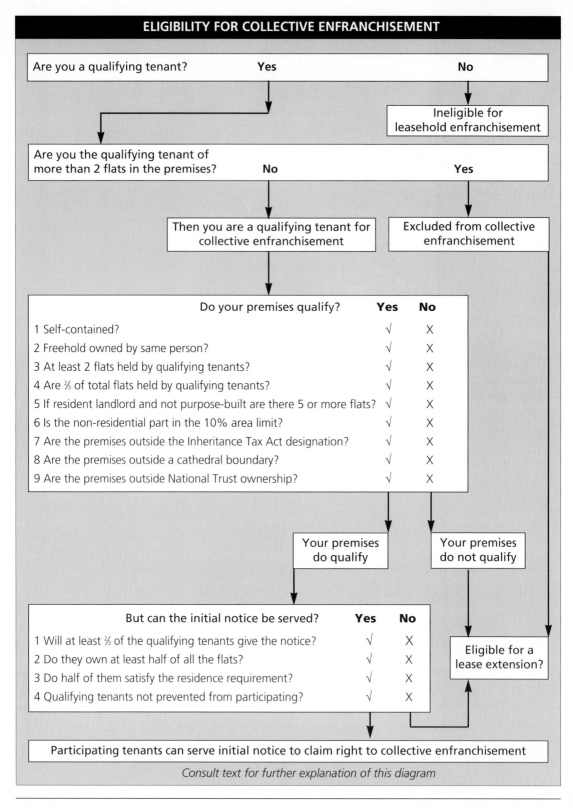

ELIGIBILITY FOR COLLECTIVE ENFRANCHISEMENT

Are you a qualifying tenant?　　　　　Yes　　　　　　　　　　No

Ineligible for leasehold enfranchisement

Are you the qualifying tenant of more than 2 flats in the premises?　　　No　　　　　　　　Yes

Then you are a qualifying tenant for collective enfranchisement

Excluded from collective enfranchisement

Do your premises qualify?	Yes	No
1 Self-contained?	√	X
2 Freehold owned by same person?	√	X
3 At least 2 flats held by qualifying tenants?	√	X
4 Are ⅔ of total flats held by qualifying tenants?	√	X
5 If resident landlord and not purpose-built are there 5 or more flats?	√	X
6 Is the non-residential part in the 10% area limit?	√	X
7 Are the premises outside the Inheritance Tax Act designation?	√	X
8 Are the premises outside a cathedral boundary?	√	X
9 Are the premises outside National Trust ownership?	√	X

Your premises do qualify

Your premises do not qualify

But can the initial notice be served?	Yes	No
1 Will at least ⅔ of the qualifying tenants give the notice?	√	X
2 Do they own at least half of all the flats?	√	X
3 Do half of them satisfy the residence requirement?	√	X
4 Qualifying tenants not prevented from participating?	√	X

Eligible for a lease extension?

Participating tenants can serve initial notice to claim right to collective enfranchisement

Consult text for further explanation of this diagram

Qualifying tenants and the initial notice

Faraday House is a block of twelve flats. Four flats are owned by the freeholder, Perpetual Estates Limited, which rents them out. The other eight flats are occupied by qualifying tenants, all of whom satisfy the residence requirement.

These eight qualifying tenants find out that the premises are eligible for collective enfranchisement. The eight are the only qualifying tenants. After further investigation only seven of them want to proceed with the collective enfranchisement. They represent at least two thirds of the qualifying tenants and at least half of the twelve flats. As they also satisfy the residence requirement, they can and do serve the initial notice. One of the seven qualifying tenants subsequently withdraws, but the purchase can still go ahead, and does so.

Initial notice check
- Not prevented from participating?
- Must be given by at least two thirds of the qualifying tenants, who
- Must own at least half of all the flats, and
- At least half of whom must satisfy the residence requirement

Your eligibility for collective enfranchisement – combining the tests

You can use the diagram opposite as a guide to assessing your eligibility. There is one, rather remote situation when the freeholder can defeat a valid claim to collective enfranchisement. This happens when two thirds or more of the leases are due to expire within five years and the freeholder intends to redevelop (see chapter 4, page 67).

ELIGIBILITY FOR A LEASE EXTENSION: THE RESIDENCE TEST

You must be a qualifying tenant and must pass the residence test in order to be eligible for a lease extension. Compared to the eligibility requirements for collective enfranchisement, this is the essence of simplicity. However, there are in fact some complicating factors which, in a minority of cases, can exclude you from a lease extension.

Are you a qualifying tenant?

The section at the beginning of this chapter explained the tests you must pass to be a qualifying tenant for either collective enfranchisement or a lease extension. There is one important difference between the two rights. In a lease extension you can be the qualifying tenant of two or more flats, as mentioned on page 18.

Do you pass the residence test?

You must have occupied the flat as your only or principal home for the last three years, or for periods amounting to three years in the last ten years, to pass the residence test. It does not matter if you have used the flat also for other purposes. You do not need to occupy the flat when you serve the tenant's notice for your claim to a lease extension, provided you have lived in the flat for a total of three years during the past ten years.

Are you excluded from a lease extension?

There are two situations where, despite your being a qualifying tenant who passes the residence test, you are excluded from a lease extension. These are:

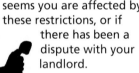

Contact your solicitor if it seems you are affected by these restrictions, or if there has been a dispute with your landlord.

○ Where your flat is within a cathedral boundary, as explained on page 24
○ In certain cases where your flat is owned by the National Trust, see page 24.

Even when you are eligible for a lease extension your landlord can defeat your claim if your lease is due to terminate within five years and the landlord intends to redevelop. This is explained in chapter 5, page 83.

Can you renew the lease more than once?

The right to a lease extension can be exercised more than once for the same flat.

Are you eligible only for a lease extension?

In some situations you do not have a choice between collective enfranchisement and a lease extension, because the premises in which your flat is situated are ineligible for collective enfranchisement. Examples of situations where you are eligible only for a lease extension are:

Premises which are not self-contained

The penthouse on top of the office block (see page 20) fails the self-contained test for collective enfranchisement because it is not divided vertically from the rest of the building.

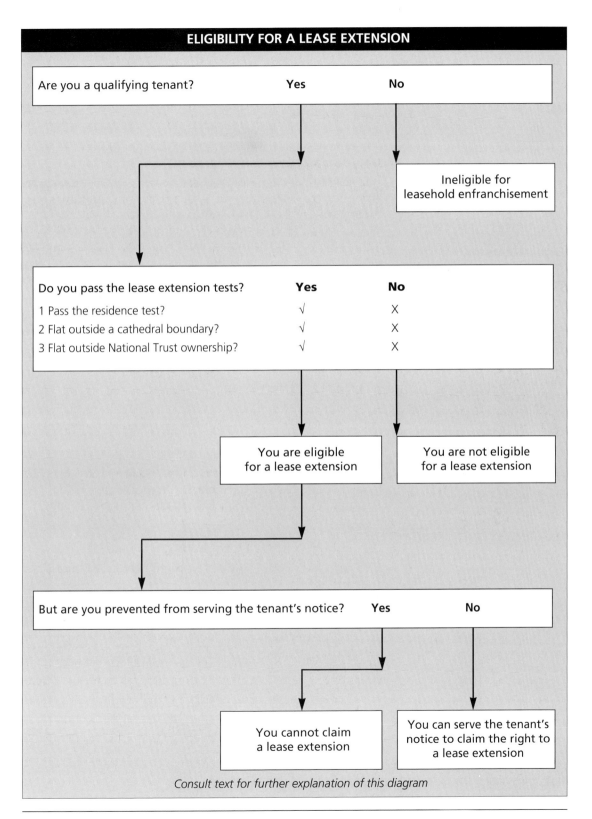

ELIGIBILITY FOR A LEASE EXTENSION

Are you a qualifying tenant?   **Yes**   **No**

Ineligible for
leasehold enfranchisement

Do you pass the lease extension tests?   **Yes**   **No**

1 Pass the residence test?   √   X
2 Flat outside a cathedral boundary?   √   X
3 Flat outside National Trust ownership?   √   X

You are eligible
for a lease extension

You are not eligible
for a lease extension

But are you prevented from serving the tenant's notice?   **Yes**   **No**

You cannot claim
a lease extension

You can serve the tenant's
notice to claim the right to
a lease extension

Consult text for further explanation of this diagram

Premises which only have one qualifying tenant

A house which is divided into two flats, one of which is owned, the other which is rented.

Premises where the qualifying tenants' flats are not two thirds of all the flats

Appearances can be deceptive here, especially when qualifying tenants, including companies, own a number of flats.

A converted house with a resident landlord and four or less flats

A converted house must have four or less flats, with one being occupied by a resident landlord, to be disqualified from collective enfranchisement. Remember that resident landlords include their children over eighteen and their in-laws.

A mixed residential and commercial development

If the shops or other non-residential parts exceed ten per cent the building will be disqualified.

Can you be eligible but be prevented from claiming the lease extension?

You make your claim to a lease extension by serving a tenant's notice. The Act prevents you from serving a tenant's notice when:

○ You have terminated your lease.

○ Your landlord has given you certain types of notice as specified in the Act terminating your lease.

○ You have to give up your flat because of a possession order.

○ There are court proceedings under way for re-entry or forfeiture of your flat, unless the court gives you permission to serve the notice.

Your eligibility for a lease extension - combining the tests

You can use the diagram on page 29 as a guide to assessing your eligibility or you can refer to the checklist below.

Lease extension check
- Qualifying tenant?
- Pass the residence test?
- Flat outside a cathedral boundary or ownership of the National Trust?
- Not prevented from serving the tenant's notice?

THE PROPERTY ACQUIRED IN COLLECTIVE ENFRANCHISEMENT AND THE TERMS OF THE EXTENDED LEASE

This section describes the extent and nature of the property you buy in collective enfranchisement and explains the differences which there can be between the terms of your old and new lease in a lease extension.

Collective enfranchisement

What do you have to buy?

The qualifying tenants participating in the purchase have to buy the freehold of the entire premises, including all the flats, whether owned or rented, any non-residential parts such as shops and the common parts.

They also have to buy out any intermediate leasehold interests in the premises. Returning to the example of Elgar House in chapter 1, page 7, Elgar House Limited will have to buy the freehold of the block from Perpetual Estates Limited and the intermediate leasehold interest from Ransom Investments Limited.

What else can you buy?

You are entitled to buy the freehold of associated property outside the premises, such as garages and gardens, provided it is owned by the freeholder and is included within the leases of the qualifying tenants' flats. You can also buy leasehold interests in such property if this is necessary to manage it.

You are entitled to buy property such as a communal garden or yard which you share with occupiers of different premises, provided your freeholder owns it and the qualifying tenants' leases give rights to use it. However, the freeholder can give rights over this property (for example, rights of access) as an alternative to selling it.

The freeholder can require the qualifying tenants to buy enough property so that any which is left has some practical use. An example would be not leaving the freeholder with an inaccessible, useless patch of land behind garages included in the purchase.

Can the freeholder retain some of the property?

The freeholder has the right to require some of the property to be leased back on 999 year leases at a peppercorn rent where:

○ It is not let to people who are qualifying tenants, such as commercial tenants or residential tenants who rent.

○ The freeholder satisfies the rules for being a resident landlord (see page 22) and is the qualifying tenant of a flat in the premises. This could happen in a purpose-built block or in a conversion with more than four flats. If the conversion had four flats or less it would not be eligible for collective enfranchisement because of the resident landlord rule explained on page 22.

○ The freeholder is a public sector landlord who lets some of the flats on secure tenancies or, in some situations, where the freeholder is a housing association.

Can the freeholder impose restrictions on the property sold?
Restrictive covenants can be imposed on a property which is sold to protect the freeholder's other property. However, these covenants cannot restrict the use of the property more than the leases have done in the past. A freeholder who owned adjacent property might impose restrictive covenants about the appearance of a building which was collectively enfranchised.

The example below shows the property which could be acquired, and leased back, in collective enfranchisement.

EXAMPLE

Elgar House acquired with a leaseback
Elgar House, referred to earlier, contains 25 flats, a kiosk, and a block of garages leased to the flat owners. The basement store rooms are leased to the tenants and there is a small communal garden area by the garages. The freeholder, Perpetual Estates Limited, owns an adjacent block of flats. The situation here is that:

○ The qualifying tenants have to buy all of Elgar House with its 25 flats, kiosk and basement store rooms. Their purchase comprises Perpetual Estates Ltd's freehold and Ransom Investments Ltd's intermediate leasehold interest.

○ They can buy the garages and communal garden and, in this case, they do.

○ Perpetual Estates Ltd takes a leaseback of the two flats occupied by tenants who rent – but not of the kiosk. The right to a leaseback cannot be exercised by the intermediate landlord, Ransom Investments Ltd. The qualifying tenants are delighted by the leaseback, because it reduces the purchase price considerably.

○ Perpetual Estates imposes restrictive covenants in favour of its adjacent block of flats to ensure Elgar House is properly maintained and decorated and to make sure the garages are used only as private garages for occupiers of Elgar House.

Extent of property in collective enfranchisement check
- Must buy freehold of entire premises and any intermediate leasehold interests
- Can buy adjacent or shared property such as garages or shared gardens
- Freeholder can impose restrictive covenants

Lease extension

The property included in your new lease will be the same as in the old lease, except that:
○ Alterations made to the flat since the old lease was granted, such as an extension, will be included.
○ Property included in the old lease but which is outside the flat, such as a garage, will be omitted.

The terms of the new lease do not have to be identical to the old lease. New terms can be imposed for reimbursement of the landlord's costs through a service charge. Under the old lease the flat owner might not have been responsible for any service charge contributions at all. Deficiencies in the old lease, such as a fixed service charge contribution, can be remedied in the grant of the new lease.

CHOOSING BETWEEN COLLECTIVE ENFRANCHISEMENT AND A LEASE EXTENSION

As an individual you may have a choice whether to join in a claim for collective enfranchisement or to claim a lease extension. Before you make your choice, you should read chapter 3 which deals with savings, benefits, costs and valuations. In coming to your decision you should also consider the following points:
○ In some circumstances your share of the cost of collective enfranchisement may not be significantly more expensive than a lease extension. The added advantage is that it gives you control of the property. The disadvantages are that it is usually more complicated and you are reliant on other flat owners for its success.
○ If you want to acquire the freehold collectively you should make sure that collective enfranchisement really

Consult your valuer and solicitor about the best strategy for acquiring the freehold.

is the best solution in the circumstances. Would a negotiated purchase outside the Act be a better alternative?

○ If a collective enfranchisement claim is made on your property, but you do not participate, you may find that you are not able to buy into the freehold later on. The fact that you cannot compel the new collective owners to let you buy into the freehold might diminish the value of your flat, should you want to sell it.

○ If you and the other flat owners are considering collective enfranchisement, but decide not to proceed for the moment, it may be difficult to muster enough support later on.

○ Extending your lease will overcome any wasting asset problem on your current lease and should help if you want to sell your flat. The issues to be considered include whether you can afford the lease extension now, or could do so later on if your lease declines in value at an accelerating rate, and the extent to which flat values may rise or fall.

○ Flat owners could extend their leases first and then acquire the freehold by negotiation or through collective enfranchisement. The disadvantage is that this may increase the amount you pay in professional fees.

○ You cannot progress a claim under the Act for a lease extension while a collective enfranchisement claim is under way on the premises containing your flat. Any lease extension claim is suspended until the collective enfranchisement claim has been resolved.

You should make sure that a lease extension really is the best solution for your circumstances and that the timing is right. Consult a valuer.

TIP

Freeholders who are faced with a barrage of lease extension claims might decide to offer the freehold to the flat owners concerned.

HINTS AND TACTICS

This section explains some options for qualifying tenants and others.

Qualifying tenants who are eligible for collective enfranchisement but who do not want to participate

If your neighbours in the property make a claim for collective enfranchisement, but as an individual you do not want to join in, you may be able to safeguard your position. For example, you may be able to agree with those who are involved that, later on, they will let you become one of the new collective owners of the freehold. The implications of such agreements are discussed in chapter 3, page 42.

Premises which are not eligible for collective enfranchisement

You could investigate whether the freeholder will negotiate a voluntary sale of the freehold. Many flat owners have acquired their freeholds in this way. The Landlord and Tenant Act, 1987, gives some flat owners the right of first refusal when their landlord wants to sell their freehold or leasehold interest.

Alternatively, you could enquire if the freeholder would sell a very long lease of the whole building. Depending on the terms negotiated, this should at least give you control of its maintenance and management, and enable you to grant extended leases.

Flat owners and others who are not eligible for collective enfranchisement

You may live in a building where a claim is being made for collective enfranchisement but, because you are not a qualifying tenant, you are unable to join in. You could ask the participating tenants if you could later on become one of the new collective owners of the freehold. They may welcome this suggestion, because it should reduce their costs.

Flat owners who are not eligible for lease extensions

Your landlord may be willing to negotiate a lease extension even if you are not eligible under the Act.

CHAPTER 3

Savings, Benefits, Costs and Valuations

If you are eligible for collective enfranchisement or a lease extension you will want to know how much it will cost. Will it save you money in the longer term? Is it worth it? This chapter describes how to answer these kinds of questions.

This chapter deals with:
- The cost of not owning the freehold
- Savings and benefits
- Purchase price and other costs
- Valuations
- Comparing savings, benefits and costs

THE COST OF NOT OWNING THE FREEHOLD

Not owning the freehold can be expensive and frustrating. You can find yourself paying high service charges without being able to control the maintenance or management of the building. Some freeholders provide a cost-effective service, but many do not. There is no reason why flat owners could not provide an equally good service for themselves.

A surprisingly high percentage of freeholders, 35% according to the Consumers' Association's 1991 survey referred to earlier, do not carry out any maintenance or request any service charge payments. Many flat owners carry out works which legally are the freeholder's responsibility. The costs you incur by not owning your freehold are examined below.

Ground rents

Although most ground rents are less than £100 per year, some, particularly in central London, are considerably more. If you do not pay the ground rent your landlord could forfeit your lease.

The freeholds of some blocks of flats, and houses converted into flats, are sold on multiples of their ground rents. This occurs mainly when the leases are fairly long and there is little or no prospect of increasing the income, obtaining capital sums from extending leases, or selling flats to sitting tenants. Properties like this are usually sold at between seven to ten times the total annual ground rent. This means that if you stay in your flat for a number of years you could end up paying the capital value of your ground rent several times over.

The examples below of London freeholds sold at auctions illustrate this.

EXAMPLE: Freeholds sold by their ground rents

Property	Date of sale	Sale price	Ground rent multiple paid
St James Road 4 flats on 99 year leases from 6/92 Total ground rent £400 pa.	5/93	£3,900	9.75
Lancaster Avenue 3 flats on 99 year leases from 12/84 Total ground rent £75 pa.	7/93	£750	10
Crockerton Road 5 flats on 99 year leases from 12/86 Total ground rent £500 pa.	7/93	£3,500	7
These are real, not fictitious, examples.			

High service charges

Despite the protection given by the 1987 and 1988 Landlord and Tenant Acts, as amended by this Act, high service charge costs remain flat owners' most common complaint. These Acts have improved the flat owners' legal position, but not owning the freehold still places them at a practical disadvantage.

○ Even a well-meaning freeholder or managing agent does not spend much time trying to save money on the service charges. There is little incentive to do so.

○ Although the freeholder has to tender the repair works to two contractors, the flat owners may know others who could provide an equal, if not better service, at a lower price.

○ The law does allow persons or companies connected with the freeholder to carry out service charge works.

The law only says that, where estimates are required, one must be from a person wholly unconnected with the landlord. This does not prevent an unscrupulous freeholder seeking one tender from a connected company and another from a contractor known to be more expensive.

○ The freeholder is often permitted under the leases to charge management fees. More cynical flat owners might argue that the 'management' provided by their freeholder actually increases service charges. If you own the freehold, you can manage the property yourself at no cost, or choose your own managing agent, who may well be cheaper.

○ It can be both time-consuming and difficult to enforce the legal protection of your rights as leaseholder.

Lack of control

Not owning the freehold means you can only influence, but cannot control, the extent, timing and cost of repair works. If the roof needs repairing, the freeholder may decide to renew, whereas the flat owners may prefer to patch it and renew later. When the flat owners own the freehold, they can decide what their priorities are.

Some leases prevent you carrying out alterations, such as changing the type of windows to ones which are less expensive to maintain, without the freeholder's permission. Certain freeholders are particularly restrictive about alterations, for what appears to the flat owner to be no good reason. The freeholder can also charge fees (which they can be entitled to do) for issuing the consent and supervising the work.

Insurance costs

Responsibility for insuring the building usually rests with the freeholder. Flat owners who own their own freehold can often achieve substantial savings on insurance compared with those who do not own the freehold. They are certainly in a better position in the event of a claim.

○ Absentee freeholders have little financial incentive to find the most cost-effective insurance. Premiums vary considerably between insurance companies. Some freeholders receive commission, at rates of between 16-20% of the premium. Your freeholder may be tempted to select the insurance which provides the best commission, not that which gives you the best terms.

○ Your insurance charges may include the freeholder's fees for the annual insurance valuation. It is advisable to have a professional valuation but you can achieve savings by shopping around for fee quotes. You may not need a professional valuation every year.

○ Your freeholder may mishandle the insurance claim, causing you and the other flat owners a loss. You may prefer to deal with the claims yourself, appointing someone on your behalf if necessary. Subsidence claims in particular can be difficult and, if they are not handled carefully and successfully resolved, the value of the flat could fall leaving it unsaleable at a decent price.

Diminishing lease length ... wasting asset

The number of years which a lease has to run affects its value. There is no doubt that, leaving aside any effect the Act may have, a 40 year lease and a 125 or 999 year lease of the same flat have different values.

It is difficult to identify the turning point when a lease starts to decline in value and becomes a wasting asset. In general terms, a flat lease's value starts to decline perceptibly from around the 90 to 80 year mark, with the decline being more marked after 70 years. There are, however, considerable variations, and valuers frequently disagree over this issue.

The Act's new rights now give most flat owners a way of dealing with the wasting asset problem.

SAVINGS AND BENEFITS

This section looks at the savings and benefits which can be obtained through collective enfranchisement and lease extensions.

Collective enfranchisement – savings and benefits

Collective enfranchisement can bring significant savings. The actual savings will, of course, depend on your circumstances and how rigorously you and the other collective owners look for ways to reduce costs.

Ground rent

The price you pay for collective enfranchisement includes the capital value of the ground rents. In most cases you should therefore achieve savings within ten years. After collective enfranchisement has taken place, the collective owners of the freehold can reduce the ground rents to a peppercorn, or they can continue with the same ground rents but use the income to reduce the service charge costs.

Consult your solicitor if you want to reduce the ground rent, or change any other lease terms.

Service charges

The flat owners can often achieve immediate savings by doing some of the work themselves, such as gardening. When you own the freehold, you are in a much better position to achieve savings if major repairs or maintenance are needed.

A determined approach to making service charge savings could bring surprising results. Remember that the previous freeholder had little, if any, direct interest in reducing costs. Acquiring and managing the freehold has similarities to taking over a new business, where the incoming management often finds it can achieve savings well in excess of 10%.

Insurance

Substantial savings can be achieved when you are responsible for the insurance by obtaining quotations from different insurance companies. If you subsequently have to make an insurance claim, you can then avoid the risk of a disinterested or ineffective absentee freeholder acting on your behalf.

Other benefits

Collective enfranchisement gives you more control over your home. The collective owners can decide how the building should be managed and can establish priorities for the service charge budget. They can also be more flexible in dealing with applications for consents needed under the leases. Another very important benefit of owning the freehold is that the collective owners can grant longer leases.

Lease extension - savings and benefits

A lease extension will bring savings in the longer term by reducing the ground rent to a peppercorn. The extended lease will not give you any more control over your freeholder or landlord. You may even find that the new lease terms bring increased service charges or insurance payments, especially if you had been paying a fixed amount under your old lease.

Of course, the main benefit of a lease extension is that it eliminates any wasting asset problem on your current lease. The value of your flat will have increased, and it should be more saleable, especially if you had a relatively short lease before.

This section helps you answer the question 'What will collective enfranchisement or a lease extension cost?' Some flat owners will find that 'marriage value' forms a major part of the total cost, so this concept is explained first.

Marriage value

Apart from causing you grief when it turns out to be expensive, the concept of marriage value is complicated and is not always easy to understand at first.

The Act uses the term in two different ways which adds to the complications. The Royal Institution of Chartered Surveyors explains marriage value as 'The additional value which is created when the leasehold and freehold interests are brought together.' Marriage value is the classic example of two plus two equalling not four but five. Bringing together the freehold and leasehold interests under the same ownership creates extra value.

When flat owners purchase the freehold of a block of flats, the marriage value is the difference between the value of their new interests (their leases plus their ownership of the freehold) and the old interests (their leases and the freeholder's separate interest). The marriage value is generated by the ability of the flat owners in their role as collective owners of the freehold to grant themselves new long leases at peppercorn rents.

Collective enfranchisement and marriage value

The Act's definition of marriage value in the context of collective enfranchisement is, to put it politely, somewhat obscure. It remains to be seen how it will be interpreted in practice.

The Act's definition refers to the ability of the participating tenants to grant themselves new long leases and requires the freeholder's share of the marriage value to be at least 50%. In practice, a combination of the negotiating strengths of each party, the purchase in question and the Act will determine how the marriage value is divided.

Some of the flat owners may not join in the collective enfranchisement but may plan to become collective owners, or to obtain longer leases, later on. Before terms for the collective enfranchisement are agreed, the nominee purchaser must disclose to the reversioner, who usually is the freeholder:

○ Any agreements of whatever nature between the
   nominee purchaser and people who are not participating

> **TAKE CARE !**
>
> There could be disputes over the interpretation and calculation of marriage value for collective enfranchisement.

tenants for disposals of interests in the premises. This could include, for example, agreements to allow flat owners later on to become collective owners or to be granted new leases.

○ If the nominee purchaser is a company, any shareholdings which people who are not participating tenants have in the company, if the shareholding could be used to acquire an interest in the premises.

The reason why these disclosures have to be made is that they could affect the valuation for the collective enfranchisement. If the nominee purchaser fails to tell the reversioner about these matters before the price for the collective enfranchisement is determined, then the nominee purchaser and the participating tenants are liable to make up any difference in the price afterwards.

Marriage value will form a substantial part of the cost of collective enfranchisement in some situations. You should discuss with your valuer and solicitor the most appropriate and cost-effective way of dealing with the situation.

Lease extensions and marriage value

The Act refers in a rather misleading way to marriage value in a lease extension. What the Act means by 'marriage value' in this context is the difference in values of the interests before and after the lease extension is granted. Thankfully, the Act's actual definition of marriage value for a lease extension is relatively clear. The landlord is entitled under the Act to at least 50% of the marriage value generated in a lease extension.

Marriage value ... what it will cost you

The points to focus on are:

Collective enfranchisement – key points on marriage value

○ If your lease has many years to expiry, there probably will be little, if any, marriage value.

○ When your lease is relatively short, there usually will be the potential for generating marriage value through collective enfranchisement.

○ The marriage value relates to the participating tenants' leases, and the freeholder's share is at least 50%.

○ Expect some disputes over marriage value.

Lease extension – key points on marriage value
- In most cases the shorter the existing lease the greater will be the marriage value generated by the lease extension.
- The landlord's share is at least 50%.
- Expect some disputes over marriage value.

Collective enfranchisement – purchase price and associated costs

The Act prescribes how the purchase price is to be calculated and makes your nominee purchaser responsible for the freeholder's and others' costs. There are four elements in the total cost.

1 The purchase price
This consists of:
- The price for the freehold of the premises.
  The price will be the value to the freeholder of all the flats and any non-residential parts, such as shops. The purchase price will include the freeholder's share of any marriage value generated. In some cases the freeholder may be entitled to compensation for loss of development value or loss which the collective enfranchisement causes to the freeholder's other property, such as an adjacent plot of land or block of flats.
- The price for intermediate leasehold interests.
  The freeholder may have granted a long lease of the premises to an investor, as in the example of Ransom Investments Ltd in chapter 1, page 7. These intermediate leasehold interests have to be purchased along with the freehold and their value established in accordance with the Act.
- The price payable for other interests.
  These are the parts of the property which you can but do not have to buy, as explained in chapter 2, page 31. They would include, for example, garages adjacent to the premises.

The purchase price will take into account any agreements or shareholding disclosed by the nominee purchaser to the reversioner, as explained on page 42.

2 Freeholder's and other relevant landlords' costs
Your nominee purchaser will have to pay the reasonable costs of the freeholder and other relevant landlords, such as

TIP

Fortunately, the Act limits responsibility for the freeholder's and relevant landlords' costs to specific items, the cost of which has to be reasonable. The nominee purchaser's liability for these costs starts when the initial notice is served.

an intermediate leaseholder. The costs are those of:

○ Reasonably investigating the eligibility of the participating tenants' claim in their initial notice and questions arising from that notice
○ Deducing title to the property interests
○ Making copies which the nominee purchaser requires
○ Valuations
○ The conveyance.

3 Amounts due by tenants
You will also have to pay any unpaid rent, service charge or related sums. The collective owners may be able to recover these later.

4 Participating flat owners' costs
Your own costs will include your legal, valuation and negotiation fees and other costs you incur, such as setting up a limited company to own the freehold.

The example below puts some flesh on the bones of how the purchase price and other costs could work out in practice.

EXAMPLE

Ramillies Road: Analysing the cost of collective enfranchisement
204 Ramillies Road is a large detached converted house divided into six flats, five of which have been sold on long leases which have 68 years to run.

The garden is shared among all the flats and there are two garages which are included within the leases of the larger flats. The freeholder, Perpetual Estates Limited, rents out the sixth flat on a short term basis. There are no intermediate landlords. Perpetual Estates does not own any adjacent property, nor is there any development value.

The five flat owners are in dispute with Perpetual Estates over the installation of a new drain and have not paid their service charges for six months. They acknowledge the money is probably due, but will not pay until Perpetual Estates' managing agent satisfies them that the new drain is working properly.

Prompted by similar problems in the past, the five flat owners decide to collectively enfranchise. They form a limited company, 204 Ramillies Road Ltd, to act as the nominee purchaser and the eventual owner. Their surveyor advises that the purchase price and other costs will consist of:

1 The purchase price of 204 Ramillies Road

○ The first component is the price for the freeholder's interest in the premises at 204 Ramillies Road. This consists of the value to the freeholder of the six flats and the freeholder's share of the marriage value generated when the five flat owners acquire the freehold and are in a position to grant themselves longer leases. The price also includes the value to Perpetual Estates of the rented flat. This is let on a short term basis, with no security of tenure, so the value will be close to the vacant possession value.

○ The second component is the price for the two garages which the participating tenants decide to buy.

2 Freeholder's and others' costs

These are Perpetual Estates' reasonable fees for employing a valuer and a solicitor.

3 Amounts due from the tenants

The service charge arrears, and any other outstanding amounts to the date of the sale will come under this heading.

4 Participating flat owners' costs

These consist of all their legal, valuation and negotiation costs, including setting up 204 Ramillies Road Ltd.

Collective enfranchisement – purchase price and associated costs check
- Purchase price:
  freehold
  intermediate leaseholds
  other interests
- Freeholder's and other relevant landlords' costs
- Amounts due by tenants
- Participating flat owners' costs

Collective enfranchisement – how to assess your total cost

You will have to assess the total cost to establish whether collective enfranchisement is worthwhile. A method you can use is shown opposite. You will, of course, have to adapt it to your own situation and professional advice will be needed to assess some costs.

The first stage should be to assess the total cost for all the participating tenants. Afterwards, you will have to apportion the costs among the participating tenants. This apportionment should reflect the variability of some of these costs. Marriage values, for example, may vary significantly between one flat and another.

Collective enfranchisement: cost checklist

1   *Purchase price*
1.1 Price of freehold
1.2 Price of intermediate leaseholds
1.3 Price of other interests
1.4 Stamp duty and land registry fees
1.5 VAT and contingency

2   *Freeholder's and other relevant landlords' costs*
2.1 Freeholder's costs – legal, surveyors
2.2 Other landlords' costs – legal, surveyors
2.3 Photocopying leases, etc.
2.4 VAT and contingency

3   *Amounts due by tenants*
3.1 Owed to freeholder
3.2 Owed to others
3.3 Interest on late payments and VAT

4   *Participating flat owners' costs*
4.1 Legal fees:
    general advice on the purchase
    establishing the company or trust
4.2 Surveyor's fees:
    valuation
    negotiation and advice
    survey
4.3 Copying leases, etc.
4.4 Accountancy and tax advice
4.5 Contingency, such as leasehold valuation tribunal and court costs
4.6 VAT

5   *Total cost*

Lease extension – price of the premium and other costs

The Act prescribes how the price of the premium payable to the landlord for the new lease is to be calculated and how any payments due to intermediate leaseholders are to be assessed. The qualifying tenant is also responsible for the relevant landlords' and others' costs. The premium and other costs which make up the total cost are explained below.

1 Premium to the landlord

This is calculated in three parts.

○ The first is the decrease in the value of the landlord's interest in the tenant's flat.

○ The second is the landlord's share of marriage value.

○ Third, there is compensation which may be due for loss of development value and any loss which the lease extension causes to property owned by the landlord outside the tenant's flat.

2 Amounts to owners of intermediate leasehold interests

An intermediate leaseholder whose lease was not long enough to grant the extended lease would be included in this category. The amount payable to an intermediate landlord is based on:

○ First, the decrease in the value of its leasehold interest in the qualifying tenant's flat.

○ Second, any compensation due for loss of development value and any loss which the lease extension causes to property owned by the intermediate leaseholder outside the tenant's flat.

3 Amounts due by the qualifying tenant

The qualifying tenant will have to pay any rent, service charge or other items due under the lease.

4 Relevant landlords' and others' costs

You will have to pay the reasonable costs of the landlord, intermediate leaseholders and third parties to the existing lease from the time you serve your tenant's notice claiming the lease extension. The costs are those of :

○ Reasonably investigating the tenant's right to the new lease

○ Valuing the tenant's flat

○ Granting the new lease.

5 The qualifying tenant's costs

Your legal, surveyor's and other costs.

TIP

The Act limits your responsibility for the relevant landlords' and others' costs connected with your lease extension. Only certain types of cost are applicable and the amounts have to be reasonable. Your liability for these costs starts when you serve the tenant's notice.

Lease extension - premium, other amounts and costs check
- Premium payable
- Amounts to intermediate leaseholders
- Amounts due by qualifying tenant
- Relevant landlords' and others' costs
- Qualifying tenant's costs

The example below shows how the premium and other costs for a lease extension could work out in practice.

EXAMPLE

Analysing the cost of Mr Armstrong's lease extension

25 Acacia Street, Ealing, is a detached Victorian house converted into three flats. Two flats were sold on leases which now have 59 years to expiry, at ground rents of £50 per year. They are now owned by a Mr Armstrong and a Mrs Hendy, both of whom have lived there continuously for more than three years. The third flat is occupied by the freeholder, Mrs Tate, who purchased the house in 1946 and has lived there ever since.

Mr Armstrong and Mrs Hendy are qualifying tenants. They pass the residence test but they are eligible only for lease extensions. Their premises fail the collective enfranchisement test because of the number of flats and the presence of a resident landlord. There are no rent or service charge arrears. Mrs Hendy cannot afford the lease extension. Mr Armstrong wants to extend the lease before he sells the flat. He is advised by his surveyor that the premium and other costs will be made up as follows:

1 Premium to the landlord

This will have two components. The first reflects the decrease in the value of his landlord's interest in his flat. The previous ground rent of £50 is reduced to a peppercorn, while Mrs Tate's successors will have to wait 149 years before the lease expires. Secondly, he will have to pay Mrs Tate a share in the marriage value to reflect the increased value of his flat.

2 Amounts to owners of intermediate leasehold interests

None.

3 Amounts due by the qualifying tenant

None.

4 Relevant landlords' and others' costs

Mrs Tate's legal and valuation fees.

5. Qualifying tenant's own costs

Mr Armstrong's legal and valuation fees.

Lease extension – how to assess the total cost

You will have to assess the total cost, to establish if a lease extension is worthwhile. A method you can use is shown below. You will, of course, have to adapt it to your own situation, and professional advice will be needed to assess some costs.

Lease extension: cost checklist

1   Premium to landlord
1.1 Decrease in value of landlord's interest
1.2 Landlord's share of marriage value
1.3 Compensation for loss of development value or loss
     to landlord's other property
1.4 Contingency

2   Amount due to owners of intermediate leasehold interests
2.1 Decrease in value of interest
2.2 Compensation for loss of development value or loss
     to the leaseholder's other property
2.3 Contingency

3   Amounts due by tenant
3.1 Rent, service charge, etc.
3.2 Other amounts

4   Relevant landlords' and others' costs
4.1 Relevant landlords' costs – legal, surveyors
4.2 Others' costs
4.3 Photocopying leases, etc.
4.4 Contingency
4.5 VAT

5   Qualifying tenant's costs and incidentals
5.1 Legal fees:
    general advice
    grant of extended lease
5.2 Surveyors' fees:
    valuation
    survey
    negotiation and other advice
5.3 Land Registry fees and stamp duty
5.4 Incidentals and other costs
5.5 Contingency, such as leasehold valuation tribunal
     and court costs
5.6 VAT not included above

6   Total cost

Issues affecting the total cost of leasehold enfranchisement

The main issues affecting the total cost, with ways you can try to reduce the cost, are discussed below.

Collective enfranchisement

○ Marriage value

The Act entitles the freeholder to at least a 50% share in the marriage value. The total cost will therefore increase where marriage value can be generated from the collective enfranchisement. The experience and skill of your valuer and negotiator will come to the fore in the negotiations on the calculation and share of marriage value. If you appeal to the leasehold valuation tribunal, because the valuers cannot agree, you are liable only for your own costs.

○ Non-participating flats

The flat owners who do participate will have to pay the freeholder the value, determined according to the Act, of the flats where the owners do not participate. The same applies for the value of those flats to any intermediate leaseholder. The cost for each participating tenant, excluding any element of marriage value, will usually reduce in proportion to the number of flat owners who participate. But increasing the number of participating flat owners may lead to a higher marriage value. The apportionment of the cost of the marriage value among the participating flat owners will be a crucial issue. You could also investigate whether tenants who rent would be interested in buying their flats after the collective enfranchisement has taken place. You might even find that these tenants are prepared to pay more than the value of their flats which was agreed with the previous freeholder, especially if they also buy into the freehold.

○ Non-residential parts

The price will increase if the premises contain shops or other non-residential parts. A way to reduce the price is by encouraging the former freeholder to take a leaseback. If the freeholder is not interested, you could try negotiating a sale of the non-residential parts to whoever is their lessee.

○ Costs

In collective enfranchisement and lease extensions, your

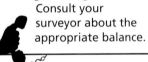

Including as many flat owners as possible in the purchase may reduce part of the price and other costs paid by each tenant but it may also increase the marriage value generated. Consult your surveyor about the appropriate balance.

TIP

If a block of flats contains a small shop which is rented out, or other non-residential parts, you may be able to sell the tenant a lease for a capital sum and recoup some of the purchase price. Consult a surveyor.

own costs, and the reasonable costs of the freeholder, relevant landlords and others, can add up to a considerable sum. You may be able to obtain fixed price quotes for your own professional fees. You could also try to obtain a fixed price quote from the freeholder or other landlords for their costs. They, too, might want to avoid a dispute about fees.

Lease extension

The main cost will often be marriage value. The skill and experience of your valuer and negotiator could affect considerably the share of marriage value which has to be paid to your landlord.

You may have to appeal to the leasehold valuation tribunal if agreement cannot be reached on the marriage value. If you do appeal, you will be responsible for your own costs only.

Fees could be another significant cost. As with collective enfranchisement, it is worth seeing if you can obtain fixed price fee quotes for your own and for your landlords' fees.

VALUATIONS AND SURVEYS

Valuations – the statutory provisions

The Act sets out how to assess the purchase price in collective purchase or the premium and amounts due to intermediate leaseholders in a lease extension. The valuer has to value in accordance with the Act in both situations and, in collective enfranchisement, a valuation must be obtained before the initial notice can be served.

Valuers could have quite a task in unravelling how much 204 Ramillies Road Ltd should pay Perpetual Estates, or what Mr Armstrong at 25 Acacia Street really should pay Mrs Tate. No doubt surveyors and lawyers will dispute the interpretation of the Act for some time to come. The unfortunate result is that part of the cost may fall on 204 Ramillies Road Ltd, or Mr Armstrong, who are responsible for both their own valuation and negotiation costs and for the 'reasonable' valuation costs of their freeholder or landlord.

The valuer must not take into account:
- Any increase in the value of the flat (or flats), if this was due to an improvement carried out at the expense of the tenant or the tenant's predecessor. Otherwise you would have to pay the freeholder, or landlord in a lease

extension, for the extra value created by tenants'
improvements.
You should discuss with your valuer what constitutes an
improvement to your flat.
○ The rights to collective enfranchisement or, in most
cases, a lease extension which the Act creates. If these
were not disregarded they could be interpreted as
increasing flat values, pushing up the price of collective
enfranchisement or a lease extension.
○ The fact that the participating tenants and nominee
purchaser, or tenant in a lease extension, are buying or
seeking to buy. The effect in valuation terms of taking
this into account could be to increase the price.

The Act has a provision which prevents the price for
collective enfranchisement or a lease extension from being
increased by property transactions undertaken after the Act
was passed.

The valuation date

The valuation date for establishing the purchase price in
collective enfranchisement is not the initial notice date but
a date agreed between the parties or determined by a leasehold valuation tribunal.

In a lease extension the valuation date is when all the
terms of the new lease (excluding the premium and the
other amounts due) are agreed between the parties or determined by a leasehold valuation tribunal.

You should take into account a rising or falling market
in your willingness, or otherwise, to agree financial terms
quickly.

The valuer's qualifications

The position differs between collective enfranchisement
and a lease extension.

Collective enfranchisement

The Act requires that the initial notice for collective
enfranchisement must not be given until a valuation has
been obtained from a qualified surveyor, who is defined as
a Fellow or Associate of The Royal Institution of Chartered
Surveyors or the Incorporated Society of Valuers and
Auctioneers.

These surveyors will have the initials FRICS, ARICS,
FSVA or ASVA after their names. (The Government can
issue regulations later which allow other people to come

within the definition of a qualified surveyor.) The Act requires that the surveyor chosen to do the valuation must be believed by the qualifying tenants to be able and experienced in valuation of this type of premises in the area in question. It is in your interest to find out, so ask the valuer to confirm this.

Collective enfranchisement valuer check
• Must be qualified, able and experienced.
• Must value according to the Act

Lease extension
The Act does not require you here to use a qualified valuer, or to have a valuation carried out before your tenant's notice is served. It would be prudent to obtain a valuation before the notice is served, especially as you are responsible for costs if you withdraw it. Regardless of who values, the valuation must be carried out according to the Act. If you are in doubt, you should use a formally qualified valuer.

Lease extension valuer check
• Choose an able and experienced valuer
• Must value according to the Act

Surveys
In collective enfranchisement the condition of the premises will affect its value and the liabilities which the collective owners will take on. It would be wrong for prospective owners to assume that, in becoming the collective owners of a freehold, they are not taking on any more liabilities than they have already as flat owners.

First, the existing flat owners' leases may not permit the freeholder to recover all the service charge costs. Second, there may be tenants who rent and do not pay any service charge contributions, with the freeholder making up the shortfall in repair and other costs. The valuation should take these points into account.

The new lease terms in a lease extension may impose a greater liability than before for service charge costs, which makes it important that the condition of the building is taken into account. Even if your liability under the new lease is not greater than before, the valuation must take the building's condition into account.

You should discuss with your valuer, and your solicitor if appropriate, the type and extent of survey which should be undertaken for collective enfranchisement or a lease extension.

Having examined the savings and benefits you can achieve and how much it will cost, the next step is to compare them.

Collective enfranchisement

The main question is: will the long term savings and other benefits outweigh the costs of the purchase?

How much will you save?

It is easier to assess the potential cost of collective enfranchisement than to assess the potential savings. Savings occur over a longer period and, to an extent, depend on the new freeholder's determination to achieve them. The assessment of savings should cover:

○ Ground rent
○ Service charges
○ Insurance

Estimates should be prepared for the total annual savings on an apportioned basis for each flat, preferably over a three year period.

How much will it cost?

The method of assessing costs described in the preceding section can be used to assess total costs for all the participating flat owners. The costs subsequently should be apportioned between the flats and, ideally, should then be expressed on an annualised basis in order that comparisons can be made on a similar annual basis with the savings per flat. If you intend to borrow the money needed, perhaps by extending your mortgage, you could use the annual loan repayments for part of the comparison.

TIP

If you are unsure about how to express costs on an annualised basis you could ask an accountant or a financial adviser.

Other items in the comparison

The comparison of savings, benefits and costs should take into account:

○ The net of tax income the freeholder will receive from flats or non-residential parts of the building which the freeholder rents out.
○ Any expenditure which the freeholder cannot recover. The cost of repairs on flats where the landlord is responsible for repairs would come into this category.
○ The cost of any bridging finance to fund service charges or other expenditure until they are recovered. Are there likely to be arrears?

- Capital payments which may be received from flat owners, or others, who do not participate in the collective enfranchisement but who later may want to purchase a share in the freehold or extend their leases. In addition, tenants of rented flats may want to buy their flats.
- Tax on receipts from the sale in shares in the company which owns the freehold, from the grant of leases at a premium, or from rental income. See chapter 7, page 100, for an explanation.

Comparing savings, benefits and costs

The comparison should be viewed in relation to:

- The increase in flat values which results from collective enfranchisement
- The increased control which the new collective owners of the freehold have over maintenance, insurance and management, with the consequent savings and benefits this can bring.

Lease extension

The main saving in a lease extension comes from the lease ceasing to be a wasting asset, possibly at an accelerating rate. The flat's value will usually increase as a result of the extension, the exception being where the lease already has a long run until expiry. There is also a direct saving from the ground rent being reduced to a peppercorn.

A detailed comparison of savings and costs would compare the cost against the increased value of the flat and the savings in ground rent. Costs which might result from higher service charges, or from other terms of the new lease, should be included in the comparison.

CHAPTER 4

Collective Enfranchisement in Practice

Collective enfranchisement can be the solution to long-standing problems faced by many flat owners. However, translating this new right into practice can give you a bumpy ride – compelling your freeholder to sell, working in partnership with your neighbours, navigating your way through a maze of complicated procedures. This chapter deals with converting your initial interest in collective enfranchisement into the completed purchase. The keys to success are organising yourselves in advance and understanding the basic procedures.

This chapter deals with:
- Who is involved
- Key points
- Organising yourselves for your claim
- Procedures for collective enfranchisement
- The purchase - legal and practical points
- Hints and tactics for your claim
- Estate management schemes

WHO IS INVOLVED

The Act refers to those who take part by their technical names, for instance 'participating tenants', 'nominee purchaser' and 'reversioner'. Your side will consist of the flat owners, referred to as the participating tenants, your nominee purchaser and your professional advisers. The other side will be represented by the reversioner and their professional advisers. The comments below expand on the brief definitions of these terms which are given in the glossary.

Participating tenants

These are the qualifying tenants named on the initial notice who are buying the freehold and other interests.

Nominee purchaser

The nominee purchaser acts as the buyer on behalf of all

the participating tenants and conducts the negotiations. The participating tenants have to appoint their nominee purchaser before they serve the initial notice. The nominee purchaser can be a person, or persons, or a limited company and is responsible for the freeholder's and other relevant landlords' reasonable costs of the completed purchase.

Reversioner

The initial notice is served on the reversioner, who is responsible for the subsequent negotiations and proceedings. The reversioner and the freeholder are usually the same but in a few cases the reversioner could be an intermediate leaseholder, such as Ransom Investments Ltd in the example on page 7.

For the sake of simplicity the reversioner is frequently referred to in this chapter as the freeholder, since in most situations they will be identical.

KEY POINTS

There are three key points which you should take into account before you make a claim for collective enfranchisement.

Freeholder's and other relevant landlords' costs

Your nominee purchaser will be responsible not just for the purchase price but also for the freeholder's and other relevant landlords' reasonable costs of the completed purchase. If the participating tenants call a halt to the purchase by withdrawing the initial notice they will become responsible for these costs. The participating tenants need to agree in advance how all the costs will be apportioned. This will apply whether the sale proceeds, whether one or more participating tenants does not take part in the actual purchase or whether the participating tenants withdraw the initial notice.

Time scales

The Act's procedures require the freeholder and yourselves to adhere to various time scales regarding the service of notices and applications to court or to a leasehold valuation tribunal. You need to know in advance what these are, so that you are not rushed into making decisions before the time limit is up. If you fail to keep to some of these time scales, you will find that the initial notice is deemed to be withdrawn, with the consequence that the participating tenants are liable for costs.

Negotiating a voluntary sale

Given the complexities of collective enfranchisement, the best outcome in some situations may be to negotiate a voluntary sale of the freehold and any other interests, provided this can be achieved on reasonable terms. But even a negotiated sale could have its share of complications, and, if the negotiations fail, you could be left with the prospect of incurring further fees for collective enfranchisement.

ORGANISING YOURSELVES FOR YOUR CLAIM

Organising yourselves efficiently is the key to success. It saves time and money and avoids unnecessary problems.

Why you need to be organised into a flat owners' group

As the name indicates, collective enfranchisement is a collective or group activity. It is your group of flat owners, not the individuals, which decides to serve the initial notice. Working efficiently and fairly as a group means being organised, listening to what others say and delegating when appropriate. The advantages of being well organised are that this:

○ Motivates the individuals in the group and helps avoid misunderstandings and disputes

○ Makes the nominee purchaser's, reversioner's, and professional advisers' work easier. This can result in lower costs.

○ Helps you plan and manage your collective enfranchisement in a cost-effective way.

The functions of the flat owners' group are discussed below.

Discovering interest, expressing views, taking decisions

The first stage is to discover if your neighbours in the property are interested. They may not have heard about collective enfranchisement or, if they have, they may not understand what is involved. You could hold a meeting and ask a surveyor or solicitor to come along to explain what collective enfranchisement is and how the procedures work.

It can be helpful to encourage your neighbours to express their views and feelings about collective enfranchisement. If they feel they are not being consulted, or their views are not being taken seriously, they may not want to join in or they may drop out subsequently.

Your flat owners' group will have to decide how to organise itself. Should you delegate some matters to smaller groups? How you organise yourselves will vary according to the number of flats, the skills and personalities of the people involved and the complexity of the purchase. Where there are only two or three flats the organisation could remain informal, especially if the flat owners know each other well. But even in a small group it would be sensible to delegate different jobs. For instance, one flat owner could assess the eligibility, costs, benefits and savings while another deals with the solicitor. A larger block of flats might need a more formal approach, with a chairperson, treasurer, and possibly even some form of constitution.

You will need to establish how the flat owners' group will take decisions on important issues. Will these be put to a vote? If so, will a quorum of flat owners be needed? Some examples of the issues where decisions will be required are:

○ Apportionment of costs

The method of apportioning the purchase price and other costs between flat owners should be settled early on. How are legal and other costs to be apportioned to flat owners who are interested at first but who do not participate in the initial notice, or to participating tenants who subsequently decide not to take part in the purchase? How are costs to be apportioned if the participating tenants withdraw the initial notice?

○ Withdrawing the initial notice

The participating tenants need to consider the circumstances in which they would withdraw their initial notice. What is the maximum which the flat owners will pay for the purchase before they decide the time has come to halt the purchase? Will the decision to withdraw the notice have to be unanimous or could it be authorised by a majority vote?

○ Ownership of the freehold

The means of collectively owning the freehold needs to be agreed. The options of a limited company and joint ownership under a trust are explained in chapter 6.

○ The nominee purchaser

Who will act as the nominee purchaser? If, for example, it is to be the company which eventually will own the freehold, decisions will have to be taken about the com-

---

TAKE CARE !

Make sure you agree in advance in writing how costs will be apportioned, whether the purchase goes through with all or some of the participating tenants taking part, or whether the initial notice is withdrawn or even never served.

---

pany before the initial notice is served. Have the participating tenants and the nominee purchaser, if different,
reached full agreement on how costs will be dealt with?

○ Non-participating flat owners
Will flat owners who do not participate in the collective
enfranchisement be allowed to become collective owners
of the freehold later on? Or will they only be granted
longer leases? The legal, valuation and tax implications
need to be considered.

○ Future management
Are there issues, such as whether to renew a roof or
replace lifts, which need to be resolved early on? Can
people afford both to buy the freehold and renew the
roof? Will the flat owners manage the property themselves or will they appoint a managing agent? This point
is discussed in chapter 8.

○ Professional advisers
Who will be appointed as the solicitor and valuer?

○ Fighting fund
How much should be set aside to cover the preliminary
costs and who will be responsible for making payments?

○ Organisation and delegation
Who is responsible for what? You will need also to
ensure the limits of delegated authority are clear.

Preliminary assessment of eligibility, savings, benefits, costs and viability

The flat owners' group needs to carry out a preliminary
assessment to see if collective enfranchisement appears to
be viable. Then, if it is, a more detailed assessment should
be undertaken before the initial notice is served.

The preliminary assessment could be carried out using
the tests on eligibility described in chapter 2 and the
method for comparing savings, benefits and costs explained
in chapter 3. A solicitor's advice may be needed on some
aspects of eligibility but you should be able to assess the
prospects without detailed advice. You will need a surveyor
to advise on the purchase price.

When the preliminary assessment of eligibility, savings,
benefits and costs has been carried out, the viability of collective enfranchisement can be established. The issues
which need to be addressed include the following, but there
may be others according to the circumstances.

○ On balance, does it seem the flat owners are eligible for
collective enfranchisement and can the qualifying

tenants satisfy the conditions required to give the initial notice? See chapter 2.

○ Are the savings, benefits and costs acceptable? See chapter 3.
○ What is the maximum each flat owner would pay?
○ Could the flat owners raise the money? See chapter 7.
○ Would the freeholder and any other intermediate lease-holders negotiate a voluntary sale, or will you have to claim your rights under the Act?
○ Is collective enfranchisement the best solution for the circumstances and is the timing right for a claim?

Managing the collective enfranchisement and the detailed assessment of eligibility, savings, benefits and costs

If collective enfranchisement appears to be viable at the preliminary stage, you will need to work out before the initial notice is served a way to plan and manage the complicated process of collective enfranchisement. One way to do this is by delegating the responsibility to specific people in your flat owners' group. Their tasks will include:

Appointing professional advisers
You will need to appoint:

○ A solicitor
The solicitor's tasks will include investigating eligibility, advising on the procedures and dealing with the purchase.
○ A valuer
If you are in doubt about who to use you can contact the Royal Institution of Chartered Surveyors or the Incorporated Society of Valuers and Auctioneers, whose addresses are given on page v.
○ A negotiator and co-ordinator
You will need someone to negotiate with the freeholder over the price and other terms of the purchase and to co-ordinate the transaction. Your valuer might undertake both these tasks, but you should find out in advance and agree their fees.

It might be worth appointing a surveyor, in addition to the valuer, to negotiate and co-ordinate the transaction for you, especially if the valuer does not want to become involved in all the details of the negotiation and transaction. Whether it is worth appointing someone separately from the valuer depends on their experience, skill and cost.

TIP

Establish whether your valuer will negotiate the price and terms and co-ordinate the transaction for you, and what the total fee will be.

Other points to note are:

○ You will need to agree your professional advisers' terms of appointment, including fees, expenses and the extent of work involved. They may agree fixed fees, in which case the work involved must be defined carefully.

○ Are the reporting lines between your professional advisers clear?

○ Are your professional advisers experienced in this type of work? Are you paying them to learn?

Monitoring progress, costs and funding

Before the initial notice is served it is important to agree with your professional advisers how progress and costs will be monitored. You need to know in advance what the next steps in the procedure are, especially when there are time scales to comply with. You also need to know whether the costs are still within your budget.

How will the participating tenants fund the purchase? If they need loans, then the initial notice should not be served until loan offers on satisfactory terms have been obtained for all those who need them.

Keeping people informed

Someone should be responsible for keeping everyone informed on progress, cost and related matters.

Estate management schemes

You should check whether an application for an estate management scheme has been made, or is about to be made. The application will, in effect, suspend the initial notice until the result has been determined. This is explained on page 74.

Decisions, decisions

Your solicitor and surveyor will come to you for decisions, for instance during negotiations on the purchase price, and they may need a quick if not immediate response. The flat owners who are managing the collective enfranchisement should be prepared to give such decisions and should be confident about the limits of their authority. There is no point in their agreeing to a revised price which the other participating tenants will not pay.

Flat owners' group check
- Discovers people's interest, enables views to be expressed, takes decisions
- Assesses eligibility, savings, benefits, costs and viability
- Plans and manages the collective enfranchisement

> **TIP**
>
> Your own professionals' fees, those of the freeholder and other relevant landlords could be a substantial part of the total cost. Giving clear instructions and being well organised helps to keep fees down.

> *TAKE CARE !*
>
> Do not serve the initial notice if there are any doubts about how the money will be raised, including the terms on which offers have been obtained.

A detailed assessment of eligibility, savings, benefits, costs and viability should be undertaken before the initial notice is served. This will cover the same areas as the preliminary assessment, referred to on page 61, but should be more comprehensive and will rely to a greater degree on advice given by your professional advisers. An outline of the issues to be covered is given below.

Detailed assessment guidelines

1 Eligibility
- Tests for qualifying tenants, premises and initial notice passed?
- Preliminary inquiries made?
- Estate management scheme application made or likely? See this chapter, page 72.
- Implications of qualifying tenants who are companies assessed?

2 Collective ownership
- Method of collective ownership decided?
- Company or trust set up?

3 Costs, benefits and savings
- Costs, benefits and savings estimated, apportioned, compared and acceptable?
- Maximum each flat owner will pay established?
- Valuation and survey undertaken?
- Tax issues resolved?
- Funding resolved with satisfactory offers obtained?

4 Flat owners' agreements in place on:
- Responsibility for and apportionment of costs for possible eventualities?
- Policy on future sales of shares in the freehold or grant of new leases? How are the proceeds to be dealt with?
- Method of future property management?

5 Organisation
- Flat owners' group set up?
- Nominee purchaser and professional advisers appointed?
- Who manages the collective enfranchisement?
- Are a negotiator and co-ordinator necessary?
- Method agreed for keeping people informed?
- Flat owners and tenants consulted?
- Way to monitor progress and costs established?

6 Negotiating a voluntary sale
- Would the freeholder and others sell on reasonable terms?

7 The collective enfranchisement solution

- Is collective enfranchisement the best solution and is the timing right?

PROCEDURES IN THE ACT

The Act's procedures are complicated and require both sides to keep to prescribed time scales. The Government will issue regulations from time to time about the workings of the Act, for example about aspects of the procedures for claiming collective enfranchisement and applications to a leasehold valuation tribunal to settle disputes. These regulations may cover topics such as proof of occupation to satisfy the residence condition, time scales for comments on the draft contract for the purchase and the payment of deposits on exchange of contracts. You need to be aware of the general content of these regulations.

> Consult your solicitor and valuer about the up-to-date position on Government regulations.

Preliminary inquiries by tenants

You may need to gather quite extensive information to assess your eligibility for collective enfranchisement and to evaluate what it may cost. For example, you may be uncertain who the freeholder is, whether there are any intermediate landlords or if some flats are in fact owned by qualifying tenants. Your surveyor will also need this information for the valuation.

Any qualifying tenant can serve a notice on the landlord, or the person collecting the rent, requesting:

- The names and addresses of the freeholder, and all others with interests in the property, including the flat owners themselves
- Details of those interests, so that the qualifying tenant can then inspect the relevant documents
- Information on whether the premises have been designated under the Inheritance Tax Act 1984, which would make them ineligible for collective enfranchisement
- Information on whether an initial notice is current. If it is, another one cannot be served until 12 months has elapsed from the date the last one is withdrawn.

Comments

Even if you appear to have all the information, it is worth asking your solicitor to make these inquiries on behalf of one of the qualifying tenants. Two points to note are:

- The landlord, or others, cannot charge for the information they provide, apart from copying costs.

○ You should make these inquiries before you assess costs. The results could affect what the surveyor has to value.

Initial notice

The initial notice must be given in accordance with the detailed requirements of the Act. These requirements include that it should:

○ Be given to the reversioner by qualifying tenants who pass the three tests described in chapter 2, page 24
○ Contain the names of the qualifying tenants, details of their occupation for the residence condition, the identity of the nominee purchaser and details of the property to be acquired including its price and other terms of the purchase. It must specify the date by which the reversioner's counter-notice is to be given.
○ Contain a statement of the reasons for claiming that collective enfranchisement applies
○ Not be served until the qualifying tenants have obtained a valuation.

Comments

It is from service of this notice that liability for the freeholder's and other relevant landlords' costs commences, whether or not the purchase is completed. Other points to note are:

○ The reversioner can require proof that a qualifying tenant does in fact qualify and must be given access to value the property. The proof has to be given within 21 days.
○ Your solicitor will register the initial notice to protect your position against any subsequent sale of the property.
○ You should delay serving the initial notice if your freeholder has made, or is about to make, an application for an estate management scheme. An explanation is given on page 74.
○ When a participating tenant sells the flat, the purchaser has the right to participate in the claim for collective enfranchisement, provided the purchaser informs the nominee purchaser within 14 days of the sale.
○ Service of the initial notice will suspend any claims by flat owners in the same premises for lease extensions until the claim for collective enfranchisement is resolved.
○ The initial notice should be prepared by your solicitor.

Reversioner's counter-notice

The reversioner must respond to the initial notice by serving a counter-notice on the nominee purchaser. The reversioner has three options in the counter-notice, which are to:

○ Agree that the participating tenants who gave the initial notice are eligible for collective enfranchisement. The reversioner must then state which of the initial notice's proposals for the purchase are accepted, or rejected, and must specify any leasebacks required. If the reversioner rejects any of the proposals, such as the price, counter-proposals have to be put forward. If terms have not been agreed two months after the date of the counter-notice, either the nominee purchaser or the reversioner can ask a leasehold valuation tribunal to settle the terms.

○ Reject the participating tenants' claim to be eligible. In this case the nominee purchaser must apply to court within two months of the counter-notice's date for a decision on whether the participating tenants are eligible. Consult your solicitor about this, as failure to apply can result in deemed withdrawal of the initial notice.

○ Either accept or reject the participating tenants' claim but also state that an application will be made to court to redevelop the premises. The reversioner has to apply to court within two months for an order to defeat the participating tenants' claim. The court will not grant the order unless it is satisfied that at least two thirds of the leases on the long lease flats are due to terminate within five years, that the building works proposed are substantial and that vacant possession has to be obtained to carry out the works.

TAKE CARE !

If you want to apply to a leasehold valuation tribunal because you cannot agree terms with the freeholder you must do this within six months of the date of the counter-notice. Otherwise the initial notice is deemed withdrawn, leaving the participating tenants responsible for costs.

Comments

The participating tenants, or at least those managing the collective enfranchisement, should meet to discuss the counter-notice and their advisers' comments on it.

If the reversioner does not serve a counter-notice the nominee purchaser can apply to court for an order, known as a vesting order, which in effect transfers the property to the nominee purchaser.

Negotiations and applications to the leasehold valuation tribunal or to court

The period after receipt of the counter-notice is likely to be taken up with negotiations over price and other terms, unless the reversioner accepts the claim in your initial notice in its entirety. The nominee purchaser may have to apply to the leasehold valuation tribunal if terms cannot be agreed.

The nominee purchaser may have to apply to court for a decision if the reversioner claims that the participating tenants are not eligible for collective enfranchisement.

Alternatively, the reversioner may apply to court to defeat your claim on the redevelopment grounds mentioned above. Either the nominee purchaser or the reversioner may apply to court for an order if the terms of the acquisition have been agreed or determined by a leasehold valuation tribunal but a binding contract has not been entered into within a certain period.

The period is normally two months from when the terms were agreed or determined.

TAKE CARE !

Ensure your solicitor reminds you well in advance about the time scales for applications to court, or a leasehold valuation tribunal.

Comments

You should ensure that your flat owners' group can respond immediately to requests by the solicitor and others. A careful watch should be kept on the costs and funding. Have all the participating tenants finalised their funding arrangements? Are they ready for the actual purchase?

The purchase

When all the terms have been settled and the contract finalised, the purchase price, costs and any other amounts due can be paid to the reversioner.

The freehold, together with any other interests being purchased, is then conveyed to the nominee purchaser in accordance with the contract. Any leasebacks which the freeholder is entitled to are granted immediately after the purchase.

Some of the more important legal and practical aspects of the purchase are considered in the next section.

Comments

You should try to obtain the solicitor's completion statement, the account which shows the amount needed to complete the purchase, as far in advance as you can. This will give extra time to arrange for all the money which is needed to be available when required. The costs of the purchase will have to be apportioned among the participating tenants and agreed by them.

Other procedural points

Some other points to be aware of are:

Claims where the reversioner or relevant landlords cannot be found

The court can make a vesting order when these cannot be found or their identity established. Your solicitor will advise on this.

Leasehold valuation tribunal and court

Each side pays its own costs at a leasehold valuation tribunal. You probably will need professional advice to present your case. In some situations the tribunal may be the only way to resolve differences between yourselves and the freeholder. Appeals about leasehold valuation tribunal decisions can be made to the Lands Tribunal.

If you apply to court, for example to obtain a decision on eligibility because the freeholder has rejected the participating tenants' claim, you could run up substantial costs without a guarantee the court will award the full amount to you if you win. Losing could leave you with a bill for the freeholder's costs in addition to your own.

Calling a halt to the purchase: the withdrawal notice

Before a binding contract is entered into, the participating tenants as a body can withdraw from the proposed purchase. This is done by giving a withdrawal notice to the nominee purchaser, the reversioner and certain other relevant landlords. Your solicitor will advise on the procedures. Withdrawing the initial notice leaves the participating tenants liable for the reversioner's and other relevant landlords' reasonable costs.

> **TAKE CARE !**
>
> Make sure that you have agreed between yourselves before you serve the initial notice the circumstances in which it can be withdrawn.

Deemed withdrawal of the initial notice

There are a number of situations where this can happen, including:

○ Failing to apply to the leasehold valuation tribunal in time when the terms are in dispute, as explained above
○ Failing to apply to court in time when the reversioner claims in the counter-notice that you are not eligible, as explained above
○ Failing to apply to court in time when terms have been agreed or determined but a binding contract has not been entered into.

> **TAKE CARE !**
>
> Ensure that your solicitor advises you in advance about the situations when your initial notice can be deemed withdrawn and the time scales which apply.

New participating tenants

Qualifying tenants who are not named in the initial notice, but who want subsequently to join the collective enfranchisement, can do so provided all the other participating tenants agree.

Nominee purchaser

The Act has procedures to deal with the replacement, retirement or death of the nominee purchaser.

Serving another initial notice

If it is withdrawn or deemed withdrawn another one cannot be served for 12 months from the date of withdrawal.

Consult your solicitor if there are, or you want there to be, changes in the identity of the nominee purchaser.

LEGAL AND PRACTICAL ASPECTS OF THE PURCHASE

Although your solicitor takes care of the legal aspects, and should advise about related practical matters, it helps if the participating tenants understand what is involved.

One point to be clear about is that the solicitor appointed by the participating tenants acts for them as a group. The solicitor is not (usually) appointed to act also for the participating tenants as individuals. You may want to obtain your own legal advice, for instance, if you are involved in a dispute with the freeholder or your neighbours.

Ownership of the freehold

You should finalise all the arrangements for owning the freehold collectively before the purchase is completed. Otherwise you will have the complications, and expense, of transferring the freehold from the nominee purchaser to the ultimate owner.

Solicitor's enquiries

The solicitor will make enquiries about the property to safeguard your position. These will include:

○ Investigating title to enquire about the ownership of the property and to see if there are any problems. This will include examining the leases to see if they all have the same terms, for example concerning the recovery of service charge costs.

○ Investigating disputes, for example to establish if there are any claims against the freeholder which the new collective owners might inherit. Any arrears of rent, service charge and insurance will be identified.

○ Investigating contracts to see if there are any which the tenants may want to take over. This will include investigating the implications for the purchase of any current building works.

Purchase report
Your solicitor should be asked to prepare a purchase report summarising the issues and highlighting any problem areas, such as where the new freeholder may not be able to recover through the service charges all the costs of repairs or insurance. The flat owners who collectively own the freehold would then have to bear the shortfall. The purchase report should also deal with the management responsibilities, as described in chapter 8.

Signing documents
Your solicitor will advise on who has to sign and by when. Delaying the purchase because a participating tenant who needs to sign is on holiday can be expensive. Interest is usually charged if the purchase is delayed beyond an agreed date.

After the purchase
When the purchase is completed, everyone in the property, including flat owners who did not participate and any tenants who rent, must be informed about the new ownership. Some people may need to be reassured about their position generally, while others may require information about future service charges or to whom they should pay their rent.

Consulting your solicitor – key issues and events check
- Your eligibility
- Government regulations on the Act
- Time scales for both notices and applications to court or a leasehold valuation tribunal
- On receipt of your reversioner's counter-notice
- Implications of your proposed purchase: the purchase report
- Deemed withdrawal of the initial notice
- Your completion statement

HINTS AND TACTICS

People and communication
Collective enfranchisement is a group activity, which makes it important to keep everyone informed and motivated. Some participating tenants may not want to take

part in the purchase if the costs increase or if they do not fully understand what is happening. One way to maintain the momentum is to appoint a participating tenant to be responsible for making sure everyone is kept informed about progress and costs.

Managing the collective enfranchisement

This can be a difficult job. The people who are responsible need encouraging and thanking. You do not want them to resign. There will be situations when it would be worthwhile appointing an outside adviser to manage the collective enfranchisement. Regardless of who manages it, there must be clear lines of communication between all those involved in the purchase.

Money, money, money

Three basic rules are:

○ Establish at the outset the maximum each participating tenant is prepared to pay and monitor the costs.

○ Agree and record the liability for and apportionment of costs.

○ Finalise how each flat owner will fund their share of the cost before the initial notice is served.

Negotiations

Negotiating can be an expensive business when you are responsible for certain of the freeholder's and others' costs in addition to your own professional advisers' fees. Your negotiators should remain flexible on the less important issues and avoid haggles. There is no point in becoming embroiled in disputes over minor financial matters if it costs more in your professionals' fees to resolve them than the amount which is at stake.

A voluntary sale

As mentioned at the beginning of this chapter, the best outcome in some situations may be to negotiate a voluntary sale. You may find that extending your lease first and then acquiring the freehold by a voluntary sale is an effective tactic in some cases. This is discussed in more detail in chapter 5, page 86.

ESTATE MANAGEMENT SCHEMES

Estate management schemes were first introduced under the Leasehold Reform Act, 1967. Part of the concern was that the newly enfranchised freeholder of a house in, say, a central London estate of terraced houses might paint the house in unsuitable colours or not carry out repairs. This understandable desire to conserve the best urban landscape, with its view of the potentially irresponsible nature of the new freeholder, masked a sharp regard for the estate owner's long-term financial advantage. Control of the whole estate, preferably by ownership but if not then through an estate management scheme, was seen as the way to maintain or increase property values. Relatively few schemes have been approved, many of these being in central London.

The Act now extends estate management schemes to properties which could be collectively enfranchised. The flat owners most likely to be affected are those in the architecturally historic areas of central London or other towns where freeholders have retained large estates. Flat owners living outside these locations, especially where their freeholder has few other properties in the area, are less likely to be affected.

It remains to be seen what effect estate management schemes will have on collective enfranchisement. They could be quite disruptive, for the reasons explained below.

The effect of an estate management scheme

Estate management schemes deal with the appearance, use and redevelopment of the properties, allowing the landlord to retain management powers and other rights over properties which have been enfranchised. The landlord in this context could be the freeholder or an intermediate leaseholder. The schemes can permit the former landlord to carry out repairs and recover the costs, or can require the occupants to carry out repairs and maintenance.

The result is that flat owners who have collectively enfranchised could remain largely disenfranchised in practice. They would still be dependent on the former landlord who retained powers over the use, repair and redevelopment of their property.

The procedures for an estate management scheme

The landlord must submit the scheme for approval to a leasehold valuation tribunal within two years of the date when the Act's provisions for estate management schemes come into force.

There are a couple of exceptions to this two year cut-off period. First, the Government has reserved the power in some cases to permit applications after the two year period. Second, local authorities or the Historic Buildings and Monuments Commission for England can in some

TIP

The landlord can advertise the scheme, as opposed to giving you notice as an individual. If you think a scheme is likely, contact your leasehold valuation tribunal from time to time to see if an application has been made.

situations submit applications for schemes outside the two year period.

The applicant must advise those who are affected by the application for the scheme and must invite them to make representations to the leasehold valuation tribunal.

The tribunal must give those who are affected by the scheme, and who are likely to object, the opportunity to be heard. In considering the application, the tribunal must balance the likely benefit to the area as a whole against the extent to which it is reasonable to impose obligations on the tenants. The tribunal also has to take into account the area's present character and architectural and historical considerations. It can approve the scheme in its original or a modified version, or can dismiss it.

Influencing the outcome of an application

There is a way in which you can influence the outcome if your landlord submits a scheme. The Act allows what it calls a representative body of people occupying property in the area, which can be a group of people in the area who are eligible for collective enfranchisement, to obtain the tribunal's permission to become involved in the application, despite the fact the application was submitted by someone else. This enables the representative body to argue the case for how it should participate in making the scheme work in practice.

The tribunal can give the representative body rights under the scheme, which otherwise would have been given to the landlord. Alternatively, it can allow the representative body to become involved in the administration of the scheme or the properties themselves. If an estate management scheme is to be approved, it is in your interest to influence how it will operate in practice.

The implications of an estate management scheme application

An application for the approval of an estate management scheme will cause problems if you decide, or have already decided, to collectively enfranchise. Problems also arise if an application is made to the Government to submit a scheme outside the two year period. The reason is that your initial notice will, in effect, be suspended until the outcome of the application has been resolved.

The Act provides that the freeholder cannot be compelled to agree terms for the collective enfranchisement until the scheme has been approved or dismissed. As a result of this and other provisions in the Act, you cannot apply to the leasehold valuation tribunal to settle the

> **TAKE CARE !**
>
> Contact your solicitor and surveyor if and when you hear about an application by your landlord for an estate management scheme. You may need professional advice to present your views to the tribunal in the most effective way.

terms, nor can you apply to court when terms have been agreed but your freeholder will not enter into a binding contract for the sale. However, your nominee purchaser can still apply to court to settle any counter-claim by your freeholder that the qualifying tenants are not eligible for collective enfranchisement.

If an application is made after your initial notice has been served, the participating tenants can withdraw the notice and, in this event, they are not liable for the freeholder's and others' costs.

Estate management scheme check
- Can apply to collectively enfranchised property
- Affects appearance, use, repair and redevelopment
- Tribunal will consider flat owners' objections
- Initial notice in effect suspended until any estate management scheme application has been resolved

CHAPTER 5

Lease Extensions in Practice

This chapter examines how to convert your interest in extending your lease into the grant of a new, extended lease. The keys to a smooth transition are preparing yourself in advance and understanding the basic procedures.

This chapter deals with:
- Preparing yourself for your claim
- Procedures for a lease extension
- Hints and tactics

PREPARING YOURSELF FOR YOUR CLAIM

Who is involved

The two sides involved consist of yourself, the qualifying tenant, with your solicitor and valuer, and on the other side the landlord, with the landlord's solicitor and valuer. The landlord is your 'freeholder' unless an intermediate leaseholder has an interest in your flat which is long enough for them to grant you the extended lease.

The landlord conducts the negotiations and proceedings on behalf of any other parties whose interests in your flat are affected by your lease extension. For example, if the freeholder is the landlord, then the freeholder conducts the negotiations on behalf of any intermediate leaseholders. The result is that your negotiations for the extended lease are with one landlord only.

The key points

There are four key points you should take into account before serving your tenant's notice to claim a lease extension.

The key points are:

Possible collective enfranchisement

It is important to establish whether your flat is in premises which could be the subject of a collective enfranchisement claim. If an initial notice for collective enfranchisement has been served before you serve your tenant's notice, or if one is served after you serve your tenant's notice, then your tenant's notice becomes suspended until the collective enfranchisement claim has been resolved. The potential for this to become a problem will increase if the flat owners do not inform each other about their plans.

In practice you may know already from discussions with your neighbours whether the premises are eligible for collective enfranchisement and whether a claim is likely. If the premises could be the subject of a claim, you should inquire whether your neighbours are considering making a claim, or if in fact they have already served the initial notice without telling you.

If collective enfranchisement is a possibility you could let your neighbours proceed with their claim and make your claim for a lease extension afterwards. Alternatively, you might decide that on balance it is better to participate in a claim for collective enfranchisement.

Relevant landlords' and others' costs

From the time your tenant's notice is served you are responsible for the reasonable costs of your relevant landlords and others. This was explained in chapter 3, page 48. Your liability continues, even if your tenant's notice is suspended because an initial notice for collective enfranchisement is served and you subsequently withdraw your claim for a lease extension.

The effect of withdrawing your claim is that you have to pay these costs, as well as your own professional advisers' fees. This could be painfully expensive so you should serve your tenant's notice only when you understand all the implications. There are situations, described on page 85, when your tenant's notice is deemed to be withdrawn. This also has the consequence of making you liable for costs.

Time scales

The Act's procedures require the landlord and yourself to adhere to various time scales for the service of notices and applications to court or a leasehold valuation tribunal. You need to know in advance what these are, so that you are not rushed into making decisions before the time limit is up. If you fail to keep to some of these time scales, you will find that your tenant's notice is deemed to be withdrawn.

Negotiating a voluntary lease extension

You should find out whether you could negotiate a voluntary lease extension. This might be a satisfactory alternative to a claim under the Act, provided the terms are reasonable. The negotiations may, however, be complicated, and if they fail, you could be faced with incurring further fees on a claim under the Act.

Lease extension – key points check
- Establish if collective enfranchisement is possible and likely
- Remember you pay your relevant landlords' and others' reasonable costs
- Watch out for the time scales
- Could you negotiate a voluntary lease extension?

Organising yourself before the tenant's notice is served

This section deals with some of the other issues you need to address. There may be others according to your circumstances.

Assessing eligibility, costs and funding prospects

Your solicitor will check your eligibility for a lease extension before the tenant's notice is served. But even asking your solicitor to do this could result in a bill. There is no point in asking for your solicitor's advice on eligibility if you cannot afford the lease extension, or if you think you can afford it but cannot in fact raise the loan you require.

Five key questions

There are five questions which you need to resolve before you ask your solicitor for detailed advice on eligibility:

- Does it appear you are eligible for a lease extension? See chapter 2.
- Is the estimated total cost of your lease extension within your budget and approximately how much will your flat increase in value by? See chapter 3.
- Could you raise a loan if you require one? See chapter 7.
- Is a lease extension the best solution for your circumstances?
- Is this the right time for a claim?

TIP

If you need a solicitor's or valuer's advice at this stage, try to agree a fixed fee as opposed to an hourly rate.

Appointing professional advisers

Before your tenant's notice is served you need to appoint:

- A solicitor
  The solicitor's tasks will include investigating your eligibility, advising on the procedures and dealing with the grant of the new, extended lease. If you require a mortgage, ask whether the building society or bank is

prepared to use your solicitor for the mortgage advance. It could be more expensive if two solicitors are involved.

○ A valuer

If you are in doubt about who to use, you can contact the Royal Institution of Chartered Surveyors or the Incorporated Society of Valuers and Auctioneers, whose addresses are given on page v.

○ A negotiator

You will need someone to negotiate with your landlord over the price and other terms. Your valuer or solicitor might do this but you should find this out in advance and agree their fees.

It might be worth appointing a surveyor, in addition to the valuer, to negotiate for you since the valuer might not want to become involved in all the details of the negotiation. Whether it is worth appointing a negotiator separately from the valuer depends on their experience, skill and cost.

Other points to note are:

○ You will need to agree your professional advisers' terms of appointment, including fees, expenses and the extent of work involved. They may agree fixed fees, in which case the work involved must be defined carefully.

○ If you have appointed a negotiator, should the solicitor and valuer report to the negotiator, or to you?

○ Are your professional advisers experienced in this type of work? Are you paying them to learn?

Monitoring progress and costs

Before the tenant's notice is served, it is important to agree with your professional advisers how progress and costs will be monitored. You need to know in advance what the next steps in the procedure are, especially when there are time scales to comply with, and whether the costs are still within your budget. You should also check that you are not prevented from serving the tenant's notice by any of the restrictions described in chapter 2, page 30.

Funding

How will you fund the lease extension? If you need a loan you should not serve the tenant's notice until you have obtained a loan offer on satisfactory terms.

Before serving the tenant's notice check
- Assess eligibility, costs and funding
- Is collective enfranchisement possible?
- Could you negotiate a voluntary lease extension?
- Appoint professional advisers?
- Work out how to monitor progress and costs
- Ensure there are no restrictions on serving the tenant's notice
- Resolve your funding

PROCEDURES FOR A LEASE EXTENSION

The Act's procedures for a lease extension are quite elaborate, in particular concerning adherence to the prescribed time scales.

The Government will issue regulations from time to time about the workings of the Act, for example about aspects of the procedures for claiming a lease extension and applications to a leasehold valuation tribunal to settle disputes. These regulations may cover topics such as deposits due after service of the tenant's notice as security for the relevant landlords' costs, proof of occupation to satisfy the residence condition and time scales for comments on the draft lease. Your professional advisers should inform you about the general nature of these regulations.

> Consult your solicitor and valuer about the up-to-date position with Government regulations on the Act.

This section describes and comments on the main steps in the Act's procedures.

Preliminary inquiries

Before the tenant's notice is served you will have to identify who your landlord is and find out whether any intermediate leaseholders have an interest in your flat. Otherwise the notice could be served on the wrong person and the valuer may not know which interests have to be valued.

You can establish the identity of the landlord and any intermediate leaseholders by asking your solicitor to serve a preliminary inquiries notice. This is served on the landlord you pay rent to, or any person who collects the rent on their behalf. The recipient must reply with the relevant information within 28 days and state whether an initial notice for collective enfranchisement where the claim is still being pursued has been received. There is little point in serving your tenant's notice if a claim for collective enfranchisement is current since it will become suspended, as explained earlier in this chapter.

Comments

You should ask your solicitor to make these preliminary inquiries early on. Unless you have details of all the ownerships already, your valuer cannot advise properly until you have the results of the preliminary inquiries. In turn this means you cannot assess fully how much the lease extension will really cost.

The landlord and others who receive the preliminary inquiry notices cannot charge for providing the information except for copying costs.

Tenant's notice

The tenant's notice has to be given to the landlord and any third party to the lease. The information contained in it must include:

○ The name and address of the qualifying tenant and the identity of the flat
○ Details of the lease and evidence that it is at a low rent
○ Information on how the tenant satisfies the residence requirement
○ Proposals for the new lease, including its terms, the premium and any other amounts payable
○ The name and address of any person acting for the tenant
○ The date by which the landlord must respond to your claim. This must be at least two months after the date of the tenant's notice.

Comments

Service of this notice triggers your liability for the costs of your relevant landlords and others. Additional points to note are:

○ The landlord has to inform you if an initial notice for collective enfranchisement is submitted after your tenant's notice has been served.
○ The landlord has a right of access to value your flat.
○ You can transfer your tenant's notice to the purchaser of your flat if you sell it after your tenant's notice has been served. The purchaser then continues with the negotiations to obtain the extended lease.

The landlord's counter-notice

The landlord must respond to the tenant's notice by giving a counter-notice. The landlord has three options in the counter notice, which are to:

○ Agree the tenant has the right to a new lease and state

which of the tenant's proposals for the new lease are accepted or rejected.

The landlord must put forward counter-proposals if any of the tenant's proposals, such as the price for the premium, are rejected. The tenant or the landlord can ask a leasehold valuation tribunal to settle the terms if these have not been agreed two months after the date when the counter-notice was given. The application to the tribunal must be made within six months of the date of the counter-notice.

○ Reject the tenant's right to a new lease, giving reasons. It is then up to the landlord to apply to court for a decision on your eligibility.

If the landlord does not apply to court within two months of giving the counter-notice, or if the landlord applies to court but subsequently withdraws the application, you can apply to court for an order resolving your claim. Your solicitor will advise on the time scales and procedure.

○ Either admit or reject the tenant's right to a new lease but state that the landlord intends to redevelop the premises containing the flat.

The landlord must apply subsequently to court for an order preventing the tenant from obtaining the new lease. The court will only make such an order if two conditions are met. First, your lease must be due to terminate within five years. Second, the landlord must convince the court that vacant possession is required in order that the building works, which have to be substantial, can be carried out.

> **TAKE CARE !**
>
> If you want to apply to a leasehold valuation tribunal because you cannot agree terms you must do this within six months of the date of the counter-notice. Otherwise your tenant's notice is deemed withdrawn, leaving you responsible for costs.

Comments

As soon as you receive the counter-notice you should discuss it with your professional advisers. If your landlord does not give you a counter-notice, you can ask the court to settle your claim for the new lease. Consult your solicitor about the procedure and time scales for this.

Negotiations and applications to the leasehold valuation tribunal or court

Unless the landlord accepts your tenant's notice claim completely, the period after receiving the counter-notice is likely to be marked by negotiations over price and other terms. You may have to apply to the leasehold valuation tribunal if you cannot agree terms.

In some circumstances either the landlord or you can apply to court for an order resolving the position if the terms of the lease have been agreed, or determined by a leasehold valuation tribunal, but a binding contract has not been entered into within a certain period. The period is normally two months from when the terms were agreed or determined. Your landlord could take you to court in this situation if you were unable to complete the new lease because you had not obtained the loan you required.

Comments

You need to be aware of the implications of your new lease terms before you finally commit yourself. You should ask your solicitor to prepare a brief report when all the terms are close to being agreed. This is particularly important if the new terms increase your liability for service charges or insurance.

Other points to note are:

○ Are you still within your budget?
○ Is all the money you need available?

Grant of your new lease

The landlord must grant your new lease when all the terms have been agreed or have been settled by the leasehold valuation tribunal or court. You will have to pay the landlord the premium, any amounts due to intermediate leaseholders, any outstanding rent, costs for which you are liable and any other sums due before the new lease is granted. Any mortgage on your current lease is automatically transferred to the new lease.

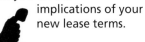

Ask your solicitor to report to you on the implications of your new lease terms.

Comments

Try to obtain your solicitor's completion statement, which shows the total due to your landlord, as far in advance as possible so that you can ensure all the money you require is available.

Other procedural points

You should be aware of the following:

Claims where the landlord cannot be found

The court can make a 'vesting order' if your landlord cannot be found or his identity cannot be ascertained. The effect is that the court grants the new lease on behalf of your landlord.

Withdrawing your application

You can withdraw your tenant's notice claiming the lease extension by giving a withdrawal notice to your landlord, other relevant landlords and any third parties to your lease. But remember this and the deemed withdrawal referred to below will leave you liable for their costs. Your solicitor will advise on the procedures.

Deemed withdrawal of your tenant's notice

There are a number of situations when this can happen, including:

- Failing to apply to the leasehold valuation tribunal in time when the terms are in dispute, as explained above
- Failing to apply to court in time for an order determining the lease extension when the landlord fails to give a counter-notice
- Failing to apply to court in time for an order resolving the situation when the court has determined the terms of the lease but it has not been entered into.

> **TAKE CARE !**
>
> Ensure your solicitor advises you in advance about the situations and time scales when your tenant's notice can be deemed withdrawn.

Serving another tenant's notice

If you withdraw your tenant's notice, or if it is deemed withdrawn, you cannot serve another for 12 months from the date of withdrawal. This could prove to be awkward, for instance if you decided subsequently to sell your flat and wanted to serve another tenant's notice in order to transfer it to the purchaser.

Leasehold valuation tribunal and court costs

Each side pays its own costs at a leasehold valuation tribunal. You will probably need professional advice to present your case. In some situations the tribunal may be the only way to resolve differences between your landlord and yourself. Appeals about leasehold valuation tribunal decisions can be made to the Lands Tribunal.

Costs might be awarded against you if your landlord asked the court to determine your eligibility for a lease extension and the court decided you were not eligible. This could be expensive.

Termination of your new lease for redevelopment

Your landlord has the right, subject to court approval, to terminate your new lease in order to carry out a redevelopment of the premises containing your flat. The court will authorise this only when:

- Your landlord applies to court during the last 12 months

ending with the term date of your old lease, or during the last five years of your new lease, and

○ Your landlord intends to demolish the premises, or to carry out substantial building works, and cannot do so without vacant possession of your flat.

Your landlord will have to compensate you for the loss of your flat if the court authorises the termination of your lease.

Consulting your solicitor – key issues and events check
• Your eligibility
• Time scales for both notices and applications to court or a leasehold valuation tribunal
• Government regulations on the Act
• On receipt of your landlord's counter-notice
• Implications of your proposed lease terms
• Deemed withdrawal of your tenant's notice
• Your completion statement
• Transferring your tenant's notice when selling your flat

TAKE CARE !

Consult your solicitor before you place your flat on the market if you intend to transfer your tenant's notice to the purchaser.

TIP

Agreeing a fixed fee with your own professional advisers makes it less likely they will spend much time on relatively unimportant issues. They cannot afford to. But do make sure they know what your priorities are.

HINTS AND TACTICS

Selling your flat with the extended lease
Your flat might be more valuable and saleable with an extended lease but you might not want to, or perhaps cannot afford, to pay for the extension. A possible way to avoid paying for the cost of the lease extension, while sharing in the financial benefits, is to find a purchaser for your flat first. You can then serve the tenant's notice and, when you exchange contracts with the purchaser, you can transfer the notice to the purchaser at the same time. This type of transaction could become quite complicated.

Negotiations
Prolonging the negotiations can be an expensive business when you are responsible for the relevant landlords' and others' costs plus your own professional advisers' fees. Your negotiator should remain flexible on the less important issues and avoid haggles. There is no point in becoming embroiled in disputes over minor financial matters if the cost in your professionals' fees to resolve them is greater than the amount which is at stake.

Extending your lease and then acquiring the freehold
The disadvantage of extending your lease first and subsequently participating in a collective enfranchisement

claim, or negotiating a voluntary sale of the freehold, is that you pay professional fees twice.

If you do proceed with a lease extension claim, knowing that an initial notice might be served, you may be able to join in the collective enfranchisement claim by becoming one of the participating tenants. The Act requires that all the other participating tenants must agree to this.

You may find that a freeholder who, under the Act, has had to grant lease extensions, decides after all to sell the freehold to the flat owners concerned at a reasonable price. When all or most of the leases have been extended, the freeholder will often be left with little or no financial incentive to manage or retain the property.

CHAPTER 6

Owning the Freehold

In collective enfranchisement owning the freehold is both your destination and the starting point for managing the property. Before you acquire the freehold you need to know if there are alternative ways of owning it and what their implications are.

This chapter deals with:
- How the freehold can be owned collectively
- Administrative aspects of owning the freehold
- Your lease after collective enfranchisement

HOW YOU CAN OWN THE FREEHOLD COLLECTIVELY

A legal structure appropriate to the circumstances of your collective ownership has to be set up before you can own the freehold collectively. There are two ways of achieving this: through a limited company or by joint ownership under a trust. The law limits the number of people who can own the freehold jointly to four. This makes a limited company the only way if there are to be more than four legal owners. It is possible for up to four flat owners to own the freehold on behalf of others, but many, if not most, flat owners would regard this as unsatisfactory.

This section examines these two ways of owning the freehold and investigates the issues which need to be resolved before the company or trust is formed.

A limited company

Many flat owners already own their freeholds collectively through limited companies. Many name their companies after the property, as Elgar House Limited has done, the company referred to in this book. Limited companies are tried and tested ways of owning the freehold. Provided the basic rules of company administration are followed, they can be a relatively trouble-free way of owning a freehold.

Your solicitor will advise on setting up the company and whether it should be a share or a guarantee company.

TIP

Employing a part-time company secretary, or seeking advice from the company's auditors, can make running the company much simpler.

When the company is incorporated, the participating tenants should appoint it as their nominee purchaser in order that the freehold, together with any leasehold interests, can be purchased by the company. The company becomes the landlord both to the flat owners and to any other tenants in the property, and is responsible for managing the property.

You will probably need to take professional advice from time to time on how to administer the company. One way of doing this is to employ a part-time company secretary, especially if the flat owners concerned do not have relevant experience. Alternatively, the company's auditors may provide assistance.

The key points you should bear in mind if a limited company is going to own and manage the freehold are:

Members and shareholders

You become a member of the company by obtaining a share, or shares, and together with the other members you have the ultimate control over the company. Members have the right to vote at members' meetings and to appoint and dismiss the directors.

Since the participating tenants' proportions of the cost of the purchase may not be the same, you will need to discuss with your solicitor:

○ How many shares should be issued to each participating tenant

○ What the company's total shareholding should be

○ What the members' voting rights should be.

Provision should be made for the future sale of shares to flat owners who do not participate in the collective enfranchisement but who may be admitted later into the collective ownership by becoming members of the company.

Limited liability

The effect of being a limited company is that normally it limits members' liability for the debts of the company to the amount they paid for their shares, provided these are fully paid up. However, if directors who are also members exceed their authority, they may be liable for more than the amount they paid for their shares.

Memorandum and Articles

The memorandum and articles control the activities of the company and its members. The memorandum describes the purposes of the company, sets out the authorised share capital, confirms the company has limited liability and describes the extent of each member's liability. The articles, which constitute the rules by which the company must operate, deal with the appointment of directors and chairman, procedures for voting, meetings and other administrative requirements.

The memorandum and articles usually have restrictions on the sale and purchase of shares in the company. A common arrangement is to require a member who sells a flat to sell their share in the company to the purchaser. This is usually linked with a restriction that a share in the company can be sold only in that situation. However, this arrangement will not be appropriate if the collective owners intend later on to sell shares in the freehold to flat owners who did not participate in the collective enfranchisement. You should consult your solicitor, and possibly a tax adviser, about how this should be provided for. The tax implications are discussed in chapter 7, page 102.

Certificate of Incorporation

This is the 'birth certificate' of the company, giving the date of its incorporation. It provides evidence that the statutory requirements for the company's formation have been met.

First directors and company secretary

A company must by law have at least one director and a company secretary. When the company is formed, there may be only one or two directors and the company secretary. Additional or substituted directors can be appointed at the members' first meeting.

What are the consequences of owning the freehold through a company?

The main consequences are having to comply with the administrative and legal requirements which affect companies. The directors are responsible for ensuring these requirements are met. The most important requirements are:

○ Maintaining the company's statutory registers
○ Submitting the audited annual accounts and annual return to the Companies Registry
○ Advising Companies House of changes in the company's officers and constitution.

The administrative and legal requirements of running a

company include the issue and transfer of shares, complying with the way in which meetings have to be called and run, and ensuring the company and its directors act within their powers.

Failure to comply with the statutory requirements can result in the directors being prosecuted and fined and, eventually, in the company being struck off. There are substantial fines for the late filing of company accounts. In practice, getting struck off is less likely than the sheer expense of setting the situation right after it has gone wrong. Looking on the bright side, many flat owners who own their freeholds through limited companies run them without problems and do not consider themselves overburdened by the statutory requirements.

What decisions are required before the company is set up?

These include whether:

○ Membership is to be restricted to flat owners, which is the usual position

○ Members who sell their flats must sell their shares in the company to the purchaser, coupled with a restriction that shares can only be sold in this way

○ Members' shareholdings and voting rights should reflect their proportion of the total cost of collective enfranchisement

○ Flat owners who do not participate in the collective enfranchisement can purchase shares in the company later on and, if so, how the price is to be calculated

○ Tenants who rent flats will be allowed to buy their flats and a share in the company.

The flat owners' group referred to in chapter 4, page 59, could decide these issues and nominate the first directors and company secretary. Tax advice should be taken on the last two aspects in the list above.

Joint ownership under a trust

This method involves the flat owners buying the freehold in their joint names and holding it on trust for themselves as the beneficiaries. In their role as beneficiaries they own the freehold in common and in equal shares. The participating tenants should appoint the trust as their nominee purchaser so that the freehold and other interests can be purchased by the trust.

Unlike the memorandum and articles of a company, the trust deed can be a relatively simple document. It should deal with:

○ Flat owners who want to sell their flats, in which case the trust deed can require the seller's share in the freehold to be transferred to the purchaser. The deed can also prohibit any transfer except in this situation.

○ Whether flat owners who do not participate in the collective enfranchisement, but later on who want to become joint owners of the freehold, should be allowed to do so. This would be relevant if, say, only three of the four flat owners in a house participated in the collective enfranchisement. Similar provisions could be made for any tenants in the property who rent, but who want later to buy their flats and become joint owners of the freehold.

○ The possibility of absentee trustees. For example, it may be that flat owners who are living abroad cannot be contacted for decisions or cannot sign documents. This situation could be dealt with by providing a power of attorney within the trust deed.

The flat owners' group will have to decide how these issues should be dealt with before the trust deed is drawn up. Tax advice will be needed if the trust deed provides for future sales of shares in the freehold to other flat owners in the property.

The trustees can organise the management of the property entirely informally. Alternatively, they can have a legal agreement on how it will be managed. In either situation they will need a bank account into which they can pay their service charge contributions and from which payments can be made for service charge costs.

What are the advantages of trust ownership?

The advantages are that you are free from the statutory, administrative and other legal requirements which burden freehold ownership through a company. Trust ownership is also less expensive since you do not have to prepare and submit annual returns and accounts to Companies House.

The disadvantage is that you are limited to four legal owners of the freehold. There can be more than four beneficial owners, but no more than four can be registered as the legal owners. Your solicitor will advise on the implications of what is known as beneficial ownership.

If you are considering trust ownership for more than four owners some of these will only be 'beneficial' owners. Contact your solicitor for advice

This section deals with the administration of the company or trust as opposed to the management of the property by the company or trust. Company administration can be complicated, which is why it is advisable to seek assistance from an experienced company secretary. The administration of a trust which owns the freehold can be relatively straightforward.

The limited company

The directors are responsible for the company's activities and the management of its affairs. It is the members, however, who have the ultimate control and who can appoint and dismiss the directors.

The company secretary

The company secretary is usually made responsible, amongst other matters, for ensuring the company complies with company legislation, for convening company and board meetings and for issuing share certificates. The company secretary's position is crucial for the administration of the company.

> *Company secretary responsibilities check*
> • Maintaining statutory registers
> • Filing annual returns and accounts
> • Advising Companies House of changes of officers or constitution
> • Convening meetings and taking minutes
> • Issuing share certificates

The directors

The directors are collectively responsible for the business of the company. They must undertake their duties in the interest of the company and comply with the statutory requirements. It is usual for more than one director to be appointed, the directors being referred to as the 'Board of Directors'. Directors can have specific responsibilities for the management of the property, such as for maintenance or for rent and service charge accounting.

Shareholders' meetings

All the company's members can attend and vote at general meetings. These meetings are important because they provide the opportunity for members to have their say in the management of the company, to consider the annual accounts and to appoint or dismiss the directors. There usually has to be an annual general meeting (AGM) every year.

A dormant limited company

You might be able to reduce the administrative requirements of running the company by making it dormant. Your solicitor will advise whether this could be appropriate in your circumstances.

The trust

The formalities of administering a trust are, in general, less than those of running a limited company. The trustees have duties to the beneficiaries and should keep adequate accounts and records, especially as a prospective purchaser of one of the flats will probably ask for copies of the service charge accounts. Your solicitor will advise on the administrative requirements of running your particular trust.

YOUR LEASE AFTER COLLECTIVE ENFRANCHISEMENT

Collective enfranchisement does not by itself affect the terms or length of your lease. It does, however, give the collective owners of the freehold the ability to grant new leases for longer periods. They can also vary the terms of existing leases, provided the flat owners and any other tenants who are affected agree.

Granting new leases

The most common reasons for doing this are to extend the period of the lease, perhaps to 999 years, or to alter lease terms which are defective. For example, the lease terms may not permit full recovery of the service charge costs, or may only allow service charge costs to be recovered in arrears, leaving the freeholder with a cash flow problem.

Flat owners who own their freeholds collectively sometimes want to extend their leases to make their flats more saleable. Not surprisingly, purchasers are more attracted to a 999 year lease with a share in the freehold than, say, a 55 year lease with a share in the freehold. If you want to extend a lease, a new lease does in fact have to be granted. Your solicitor may advise that a new lease also should be granted when extensive revisions of the lease terms are required.

The collective owners may later on want to grant new leases to flat owners who did not participate in the collective enfranchisement, to tenants who rent but who now want to buy their flats, or to the tenants of garages or other

TAKE CARE !

Varying lease terms is a complicated business which should be left to your solicitor. The new collective owners of the freehold should not tell flat owners or others that the terms of existing leases can be ignored or varied unless this is done following legal advice and is properly documented.

non-residential parts of the building. The collective owners may have to grant a new lease if someone claims a lease extension under the Act.

The ideal position is for the collective owners to agree between themselves before collective enfranchisement takes place whether they will grant new leases, to whom, on what terms, and how the proceeds (if any) will be dealt with. This reduces the chance of the collective owners disagreeing after they have purchased the freehold about the need for, or the terms of, new leases.

When you decide to grant new leases, you should consult your solicitor about the proposed terms, any resolutions or decisions which are needed by the company or trustees in order to grant the leases, and the tax implications.

Varying the terms of leases

A frequent reason for varying leases after purchasing the freehold is to reduce the ground rent to a peppercorn. Another reason is that the existing leases may be defective, perhaps due to the service charge problems mentioned above, or possibly by requiring the landlord's consent in situations where it is no longer thought to be necessary.

Leases cannot be varied without the mutual consent of the landlord and tenant, except where the landlord or tenant obtains a court order under the Landlord and Tenant Act, 1987.

As with the grant of new leases, it is preferable for the collective owners to agree beforehand whether later on they will vary the leases and, if so, what the terms will be. There may be tax implications when the terms are varied, for example if the rent is increased.

Granting and varying leases check
- Freeholder's and tenant's consent is required unless there is a court order under the Landlord and Tenant Act, 1987
- Check tax implications beforehand
- Consider and agree the principle and main terms before collective enfranchisement. Remember that your nominee purchaser may have to tell the freeholder about this

CHAPTER 7

Raising the Money and Tax

You may want to raise the money for leasehold enfranchisement by a mortgage or an unsecured loan. Finding out where you can raise the money and assessing how much is needed is an important step on the critical path to success. However, this can be a complicated business, especially for collective enfranchisement. The tax implications of leasehold enfranchisement will not be a problem for many people, but you should at least be aware of the issues.

This chapter deals with:
- Identifying when the money is needed
- Raising the money
- Tax liabilities

IDENTIFYING WHEN THE MONEY IS NEEDED

You may need to draw up a schedule of the payments which will have to be paid during the collective enfranchisement so that you can co-ordinate all the participating tenants' contributions. This will help to ensure that all the money required is available on time.

Failure to provide all the money on time could have a worse result than merely a delay in buying the freehold. It could mean the participating tenants have to abandon the purchase and withdraw their initial notice. This would leave them with a bill for their freeholder's and other relevant landlords' costs, in addition to their own fees.

Identifying when the money will be needed in a lease extension is not so complicated, but planning ahead does help to avoid unpleasant surprises.

The schedule of payments for collective enfranchisement
Payments will become due in three stages.

Stage one – Preliminary assessment
The preliminary assessment of eligibility, savings, benefits,

costs and viability for collective enfranchisement (see page 61) could run up some costs, mainly for legal and valuer's fees. The assessment for a lease extension (see page 79) could also incur similar costs.

Stage two – Detailed assessment
The detailed assessment prior to serving the initial or the tenant's notice (see pages 62 to 65) will incur further costs, again mostly in professional fees. In collective enfranchisement there could be the cost of setting up the limited company or trust to own the freehold. Tax advice may also be required at this stage.

Stage three – Purchase of the freehold or grant of the extended lease
The majority of payments will become due at this, the final stage. You can estimate the likely payments by using the methods for assessing total costs described on pages 47 and 50. Nearer to the time of purchase, your solicitor's completion statement will bring you up to date with most, if not all, of the payments due at this stage.

The two points below apply to collective enfranchisement only.

○ It is worth setting up a fighting fund for the cost of the preliminary and detailed assessments. Otherwise one or more flat owners may have to foot the bills and recover the money from the remainder.

○ The flat owners' group should appoint someone to schedule the payments, to identify and help resolve any problems in raising the total money required, and to ensure that all the money is available on time. If problems in raising the money cause some participating tenants to pull out from the purchase, those who remain will have to shoulder an extra share of the cost, unless they all pull out.

Identifying when the money is needed check
• Draw up a schedule of payments
• Set up a fighting fund
• Appoint someone to co-ordinate the participating tenants' contributions

RAISING THE MONEY

You may want to raise money through a mortgage or an unsecured loan. It is difficult to generalise about building societies' and banks' attitudes to leasehold enfranchisement. Many are willing to lend in principle, subject to the status of the borrower and adequate security. It could become a valuable source of business for them.

Some building societies and banks may lend to the limited company which owns the freehold, as opposed to providing individual mortgages or loans for each of the participating tenants. This would make raising the money for collective enfranchisement much less complex than each participating tenant trying to raise individual loans separately – and, possibly, from different sources.

There could, however, be legal and practical problems in this approach, so discuss the implications with your solicitor first. On the other hand it could be difficult to co-ordinate a series of individual mortgage or loan transactions to ensure all the money is available on time.

Negative equity

The spectre of 'negative equity', when the amount of your existing loan exceeds the value of your flat, may affect some flat owners who want to borrow. It can be difficult, but not always impossible, to obtain loans in this situation.

Leasehold enfranchisement might in some circumstances turn out to be a solution to the problem. This is due to the increase in the value of the flat which can be generated by a lease extension or by becoming one of the collective owners of the freehold. Collective enfranchisement or a lease extension might therefore release you from the negative equity trap, enabling you to sell your flat.

Obtaining a mortgage

The points below apply to both collective enfranchisement and lease extensions.

Will the amount you need change?

You can estimate the total cost, using the methods described in chapter 3, but it is difficult to be precise about the amount you will need eventually. The final price probably will not be the same as the amount quoted in your initial or tenant's notice. Your share of the cost in collective enfranchisement may increase if other participating tenants pull out from the purchase, or decrease if others join in. One solution would be to establish the maximum the building society or bank would lend and request your mortgage for that amount, knowing the full extent might not be taken up.

Can you provide security?

Unless you can offer adequate security you may not be able to obtain the mortgage advance you require. This problem could arise even if you have adequate security now, since at first it may appear to the lender that the amount you are asking for will exceed the level of security which the lender requires. If there appears to be a problem, explain the valuations of your flat before and after the proposed lease extension or collective enfranchisement to the building society or bank. They may not have appreciated the extent to which your flat could increase in value as a result.

What conditions will the mortgage offer have?

You should establish the likely conditions of the mortgage offer before you send in the mortgage application form and your cheque for any administration fee. How long will the offer remain open for, what are the valuation and survey requirements and what conditions will have to be satisfied before the money is released? You should find out whether the lender will use your solicitor for the mortgage advance.

If your collective enfranchisement will be financed by individual mortgages, you should ensure that all the mortgage offers have been received and are satisfactory before the initial notice is served. If you need a mortgage for your lease extension, you should also ensure that the mortgage offer is satisfactory before you serve your tenant's notice.

An unsecured loan

An alternative to a mortgage, especially for relatively small amounts, is a loan which is not secured by a mortgage. Unsecured loans are usually simpler to arrange than mortgages, but interest rates are higher and repayment periods are shorter. Banks, building societies and finance companies all provide unsecured loans.

TIP

Try to find out in advance what the mortgage offer conditions will be. If they are unacceptable you can at least save your mortgage application fee and other expenses by not applying.

Raising the money check
- Remember the amount you need may change
- Identify the mortgage offer conditions in advance
- Ensure mortgage offers are satisfactory before the initial or tenant's notice is served

TAX

Tax is used here in its broadest sense to include:
○ Capital gains tax
○ Corporation and income tax on ground rents and interest receivable
○ Stamp duty
○ VAT

While you should recognise the potential tax implications of collective enfranchisement and lease extensions, it is important to keep this in perspective. Many flat owners already have collectively purchased their freeholds without running into tax problems as a result of the purchase, or subsequently while managing the property. Lease extensions do not normally have tax implications, apart from stamp duty and VAT on professional fees.

This section gives an outline of the current position on tax.

TIP

The Inland Revenue and Customs and Excise provide free advice and publications on tax and VAT.

Lease extensions

You should note the following:

○ Stamp duty at 1% will be due when the new lease is granted, if the premium and amounts to intermediate leaseholders exceed £60,000.

○ If you raise the money by a mortgage, tax relief on mortgage payments up to the current limit should be available provided the flat is your principal private residence.

○ VAT will not be payable on the premium and amounts due to intermediate leaseholders, but you will have to pay VAT on your own professional fees and your landlord's and others' reasonable costs.

Collective enfranchisement

The tax implications of collective enfranchisement may be more substantial. They should always be considered before the initial notice is served, and before the limited company or trust which will own the freehold, is formed. There are not normally tax complications when all the occupiers in the building participate in the collective enfranchisement. Tax and other complications can arise when some occupiers of the building, who may own or rent flats or even shops, do not or cannot participate. For instance:

○ Ground or other rents received by the freeholder from these occupiers can be liable to tax.

○ The collective owners may later want to admit flat owners who did not participate in the collective enfranchisement into the collective ownership of the freehold.

○ The grant of new leases for premiums can result in a tax liability for the company or trust.

The main situations where there are potential tax liabilities are as follows:

Acquiring the freehold

Your solicitor, and possibly a tax adviser, should advise on the tax aspects of collectively owning the freehold in your circumstances. The structure of the company or trust that you set up may have to be adjusted to deal with the tax implications. You should also seek advice on how the company should fund the acquisition of the freehold. This could be by the subscription of shares or by loans to the company.

It is important to establish the tax implications in advance if the collective owners intend later on to admit non-participating flat owners or other occupiers into the collective ownership in return for payments to the company or trust. The same applies if the collective owners are considering granting them leases at premiums or at new rents. The participating tenants will probably want to find out if they can recoup their original contributions for the collective enfranchisement. You will need advice on this complicated area of tax and company or trust law.

Stamp duty at 1% will be due when the purchase price exceeds £60,000. If the property is purely residential, VAT will not be payable on the purchase price, although it may be if there is a commercial element. You should find out in advance if VAT will be payable on any commercial element, since at 17.5% of the purchase price it could increase the total price significantly and it may not be recoverable. VAT will be payable on your professionals' fees and the freeholder's and other relevant landlords' reasonable costs. You will not be able to claim tax relief on a mortgage for your cost of becoming one of the collective owners.

You may be eligible for tax relief on the interest paid on a loan to buy shares in a company which owns the freehold, provided it is a close company. Consult a tax adviser.

Selling your interest in the freehold when selling your flat

The rules of the company or the trust which owns the freehold may require a flat owner who sells their flat to sell their share of the freehold to the purchaser. In practice, the share of the freehold is sold frequently for a nominal sum, with the owner recouping the cost of the purchase by increasing the flat's price. Tax advice should be sought in advance if the sale of your interest in the freehold will result in a capital gain.

Trying to recoup the cost of collective enfranchisement by admitting new collective owners or by granting new leases, raises tax and other complications. Consult your solicitor first.

Admission of new collective owners

The most common reason for this is to allow a flat owner who did not participate in the collective enfranchisement to subsequently become one of the collective owners, either as a member of the company or as a trustee of the trust which owns the freehold. Ideally, the collective owners should have catered for this possibility before the company or trust which owns the freehold was set up. You should consult your tax adviser if you are considering this but are unsure about the financial or the tax implications. In particular, you should take advice if you are considering distributing the proceeds of the sale from the company or trust.

Granting new leases to flat owners who are collective owners of the freehold

The collective owners may want to grant themselves new leases if their existing leases are relatively short or if there are problems with the existing lease terms. New leases are frequently granted for a peppercorn rent to avoid tax liability.

Granting new leases to occupiers or others who are not collective owners

There could be a liability on the company or trust for capital gains tax if a new lease is granted, possibly as a result of a lease extension claim, for a capital payment. Such payments are known as premiums. VAT may have to be charged on the premium for a commercial lease, for example if at some stage a new lease is granted to a shop or a block of garages which are included in the freehold ownership. You should:

○ Consider the tax implications, ideally before the company or trust is set up, so that a tax-efficient structure can be achieved

○ Take tax advice before any lease is granted at a premium.

Rental income received by the freeholder

The company or trust which owns the freehold is liable to corporation or income tax on the ground rents received from the flat owners. If the amounts involved are relatively small, in practice there is often no tax liability. The collective owners may reduce the ground rents to a peppercorn, both as a convenience and to minimise the tax liability. There will be a tax liability on income received from flats, garages or other parts of the building which the freeholder rents out. Some expenses, such as maintenance provided by the freeholder which cannot be recovered under the service charges, can be deducted to reduce tax.

VAT is not chargeable on residential rents, but the freeholder should check the position with commercial rents, as VAT can be chargeable in certain situations.

Service charges received by the freeholder
When all the flat owners in the building are members of the company, or are all trustees, the service charges received by the company or trust will not normally be taxable as income. If some of the service charge payments come from people who are not members of the company, or who are not trustees, there could be a tax liability if there is a surplus on the service charge account. Interest received when service charge money is held on deposit as a trust fund is also liable to tax.

VAT is not chargeable normally on the service charges due by flat owners, but it may have to be charged on service charges due from commercial tenants. You should consult your tax adviser if there are commercial tenants.

Tax check
- Establish the tax position before collective enfranchisement takes place
- Potential tax liabilities increase when some occupiers in the building are not collective owners
- Admitting new collective owners of the freehold or granting leases at premiums can have tax implications
- Consider reducing ground rents to minimise tax
- Find out which expenses can be set against rental income
- Commercial tenants can bring VAT complications

The example below shows how some of the tax aspects of collective enfranchisement could work out in practice:

EXAMPLE

Cresswell House: collective enfranchisement and taxation
Cresswell House is a 1930s block of twelve flats overlooking the sea on the south coast. Some of the leases have become more difficult to sell as they have less than 75 years to expiry. The freeholder, Ransom Investments Ltd, and the twelve flat owners are at odds over the repairs required to the metal windows, the unreliable lift and the price Ransom Investments Ltd wants to charge for lease extensions.

All the flat owners are qualifying tenants and the premises are eligible for collective enfranchisement.

However only eight flat owners want to proceed. Eventually the freehold is purchased for £48,000, excluding fees and other costs. The remaining four flat owners hope to buy their share of the freehold later, finance permitting.

The sequence of events is that:

- The eight flat owners discuss the tax implications with their solicitor and accountant before Cresswell House Ltd is set up to acquire the freehold. In particular, they want to know how, as individuals, they might be able to recoup their initial outlay from the payments expected when the other four flat owners eventually buy shares in the freehold. They are advised about this, and about how to minimise the tax liability on ground rents and service charges.
- Cresswell House Ltd is incorporated and purchases the freehold. No stamp duty is paid since the cost is less than £60,000, nor is VAT charged on the purchase price since Cresswell House is entirely residential. VAT is charged on the solicitor's and valuer's fees.
- The eight flat owners ask their solicitor to grant new 999 year leases at a peppercorn. It appears corporation tax will be due on Cresswell House Ltd for each of the remaining four ground rents of £75 per year, but certain expenses can be set against the income.
- Cresswell House Ltd subsequently issues shares in the company to three of the remaining four flat owners who want to become collective owners of the freehold. They are charged £5,000 each and their ground rents are reduced to a peppercorn.
- The one flat owner who does not own a share in the company asks for a lease extension. Both parties want to avoid dealing with a claim to a lease extension under the Act. The extension is agreed in principle, but Cresswell House Ltd consult their tax adviser before the lease is granted to check on any tax liability on the premium.
- The service charges which Cresswell House Ltd collects in advance for the lift and window replacements are placed in an interest-bearing deposit account. This is a cause for irritation when the flat owners find tax is charged on the interest.

CHAPTER 8

Property Management

Obtaining management control can be one of the main reasons for collective enfranchisement. Managing your property well can be satisfying and rewarding, or it can turn out to be difficult and complicated. Tempers can rise. Unless the new management is well organised and aware of the pitfalls, they can end up – perhaps like those responsible previously – unpopular and criticised.

This chapter deals with:
- Management after collective enfranchisement
- Management audits and codes of practice

MANAGEMENT AFTER COLLECTIVE ENFRANCHISEMENT

This section covers the main issues you need to consider.

Who is responsible?

After collective enfranchisement has taken place the new freeholder becomes the landlord responsible under the leases for managing the property. The flat owners who participated in the collective enfranchisement do control the management, but through the company or trust which owns the freehold. It is important to distinguish your separate roles, as an individual flat owner and as one of the collective owners of the freehold. Mixing these roles can result in problems, as shown below.

EXAMPLE

Mixing your roles
This example is about 204 Ramillies Road, the property referred to in chapter 3, page 45. The five flat owners have collectively enfranchised and now own and manage their freehold through 204 Ramillies Road Ltd. One of the flat owners and a member of 204 Ramillies Road Ltd, the rather impetuous Mr Hanwell, is incensed at the delay in

repairing the roof which leaks through his living room ceiling. He instructs Anytime Repairs Bros to get on with the job, at a cost of £400.

Anytime Repairs send the bill to Mr Hanwell who refuses to pay, maintaining the order was on behalf of 204 Ramillies Road Ltd, not himself. He finds it difficult to persuade the other flat owners to pay up immediately since they argue he was not authorised by the company to place the order and should have obtained estimates. They eventually do pay most of their share but not until Anytime Repairs has taken the chastened Mr Hanwell to the Small Claims Court.

TAKE CARE !

You are not managing the property as an individual but on behalf of the company or trust which owns the freehold. Make sure orders are in the company's or trust's name.

You may wonder who is legally responsible if you appoint a managing agent to look after the property. In general terms, the answer is that the freeholder is still legally responsible for the management of the property, because the managing agent is acting on behalf of and to the instructions of the freeholder. There are exceptions to this, for instance, when the managing agent does something expressly forbidden or which clearly was not authorised.

Another point which is relevant here is that in your role as director of the company owning the freehold, or as a trustee, you can be personally liable for some aspects of mismanagement. For instance, company directors and trustees can have personal liabilities under the Health and Safety at Work Act to supply anchor points for safety harnesses when window cleaners are working in the common areas. This could be relevant in a mansion block. Personal liability also applies to failures to arrange regular inspections of lifts and boilers in common parts.

TIP

Managing the property in a responsible and reasonably safety-conscious way should avoid most of these personal liability problems. The law in this area has become much more complex recently so it makes sense to check with a solicitor or surveyor if you are managing a large or compli-cated building.

What you are responsible for?

The freeholder's main responsibilities are likely to be those set out below. In practice, the responsibilities will vary according to the leases.

Repairs, services and service charge recovery

Carrying out repairs and maintenance, providing services such as heating or gardening, and recovering the cost through the service charge are some of the most important responsibilities. They are certainly the most controversial aspects of property management. You need to comply with the law on service charges and to exercise financial control in order to discharge these responsibilities properly.

Complying with the law on service charges

You should be familiar with the law on variable service charges. These are payments made by a flat owner which are based on the cost of repairs, services and insurance provided by the landlord. Fixed service charges, which do not vary according to the cost of provision, are not covered by the same laws. In essence, the law is that the landlord's costs in carrying out the repairs and services can be recovered as service charges if:

○ They were reasonably incurred
○ The works or services were to a reasonable standard
○ The demand for recovery was made within 18 months of the costs being incurred.

The main points to take note of concerning service charges are:

○ If the landlord's proposed works cost more than £1,000, or the number of flats times £50, whichever is greater, the landlord must obtain at least two estimates. One estimate must be from someone who is not connected in any way with the landlord.
○ When the landlord is obliged to obtain estimates the tenants must be consulted about them. If there is a recognised tenants' association, the landlord must give its secretary a notice specifying the proposed works, together with an estimate, and must allow the association to propose another source for an estimate. Where there is no association, each tenant who is liable for the costs must be given a notice and a copy of the estimates. Alternatively, these documents must be placed where all tenants can see them. The landlord must consider any comments made, and the works should not start until after the date in the notice, unless they are urgent.
○ A tenant, or recognised tenants' association, can request a summary of the service charge costs incurred in the last accounting period and has the right to inspect documents. This summary enables tenants to see how the costs are, or will be, reflected in their service charge demands.
○ When service charges are payable in advance, the amount demanded must be reasonable. Any further service charge payments due, or credits, must be made at the end of the accounting period when the costs have been incurred.

○ Service charge payments must be held by the landlord as trust funds in a bank or building society account. This means that service charge monies are held, first, for payment of recoverable costs and, secondly, with the remainder being on trust for the tenants.

○ Tenants can challenge service charges in court, by seeking a declaration that the service charges should not be recoverable, or by defending themselves against the landlord's claim by the defence that the charges are unreasonable.

Insurance

Responsibility for the building insurance often rests with the landlord, with the cost being recovered through the service charge. The law on service charges then applies, giving the tenant the right to a summary of the insurance cover, including the amount insured, the risks covered and the name of the insurer. The insurance premiums must also be reasonable. The tenant has the right to inspect and copy the insurance policy and accounts, and can notify the insurers of claims which the tenant considers are payable.

When the landlord is responsible for insurance the items covered should include:

○ Rebuilding costs, subsidence and associated fees
○ Public liability and other possible claims against the freeholder
○ Any lifts, boilers or other plant.

> *Service charge check*
> • Service charge costs are recoverable when reasonably incurred and the works are to a reasonable standard
> • Estimates are required for works more than £1,000 or £50 times the number of flats, whichever is the greater
> • Consult with tenants if estimates are required
> • Advance payments must be reasonable
> • Payments to be held as trust funds
> • Tenants have a right to see a summary of insurance cover

Financial control

In practice, this will involve preparing service charge budgets for consultation with the flat owners, controlling expenditure, collecting rents and service charges, chasing up arrears, keeping accounts, paying contractors and banking money received. The tax and VAT implications dealt with in chapter 7 need to be considered.

Ground and other rents collected can in some cases be used to reduce the cost of service charge expenditure, so it

TIP

Check the insurance policy conditions carefully. The policy might be invalidated if, for example, you overlook routine maintenance on a boiler or a lift.

TAKE CARE !

If there is a dispute between the landlord and a flat owner or a tenant, for instance over unauthorised alterations, the landlord sometimes is advised not to charge rent since this can prejudice subsequent legal action. Consult your solicitor if there is a serious dispute.

is important they are collected promptly to help the cash flow. Rent demands must by law state the name and address of the landlord and give a UK address where the tenant can serve a notice.

Landlord's consents

Leases often require the tenant to obtain the landlord's consent for structural alterations, changes of use, or even for keeping pets. As mentioned on page 39, this can be a source of friction, especially if the previous landlord had been restrictive.

However, the landlord does need to ensure that structural alterations are safe and, in other situations where consents are requested, that the consequences will not be disruptive for the rest of the flat owners and tenants. It is best to err on the side of caution and take professional advice if you are unsure about the landlord's powers to refuse consent, or do not know whether the proposed alterations are safe.

TIP

Costs incurred by the landlord in taking advice about a tenant's request for consents often can be recovered from the tenant, but check in advance what the lease says.

Tenants who rent their flats

Where the property has residential tenants whose leases are for less than seven years, the landlord must keep in repair:

○ The structure and exterior of the flat

○ The installations for the supply of gas, water, sanitation and space and water heating.

Communication

Many problems in property management stem from, or are made worse by, poor communication. Merely following the law on service charges does not mean the landlord is communicating properly. Consulting flat owners and other occupiers about the range of management issues is essential. It will not make any problems vanish, but it will help to keep them in proportion.

Preparing for management

You should ask your solicitor to advise in the purchase report on the future management of the property. Even if the day-to-day management will be undertaken by a managing agent, the new landlord should be aware of the management responsibilities and obligations. Otherwise it may be difficult to know what the managing agent should be doing.

Before you take over the management reins, either directly or through a managing agent, you need to have a clear idea of the following points.

The management responsibilities and tenants' obligations

It should be relatively straightforward to identify these when the building consists entirely of owner-occupied flats. If the building contains a mix of owned and rented flats, or if it is partially commercial, the identification of responsibilities and obligations could be more complicated. Your purchase report should cover these issues. There may be property management responsibilities or obligations in the articles and memorandum of the company, or in the trust deed. Your solicitor should also advise on this.

Cost recovery

The new landlord must know whether all the costs of running the building can be recovered from the occupants and when the recovery can be made. Some leases only permit recovery of a fixed service charge amount, while others limit the items for which costs can be recovered. You could find, for instance, that you are able to recover management or audit fees from some but not all the flat owners. An assessment of cost recovery should be included in the solicitor's purchase report.

The landlord may be able to obtain a court order under the Landlord and Tenant Act, 1987, to vary lease terms which are defective and unsatisfactory concerning service charges, insurance and other matters. Consult your solicitor about this.

Service charge budget and expenditure

If there is a service charge budget you should check whether it covers the anticipated costs adequately. You should prepare a service charge budget if none exists.

Repairs

Repairs may have to be carried out immediately after the freehold has been purchased. Is there enough money in the service charge account?

Disputes

If there have been disputes between the previous freeholder and flat owners or tenants, or even between flat owners on management issues, you need to have the relevant papers and background information. A change of management is a good time to resolve these disputes.

Company or trust administration requirements

When the management of the building is carried out through a company, or by trustees, the company or trust needs to be administered properly. For example, if service charge increases have to be agreed at a meeting of company members, the meeting will have to be called in accordance with the company's memorandum and articles.

People, people, people

There will be times when the need to understand the management responsibilities fully, or to check if there is enough in the service charge account to pay the bills, has to take priority. But time should be found to inform and consult with flat owners, and other occupiers, about plans and priorities. This is particularly relevant when the impetus behind collective enfranchisement was to restore control of the building to those who live in it.

> *Preparing for management check*
> - Make sure the purchase report covers management aspects
> - Identify management responsibilities and tenants' obligations
> - Check if all costs are recoverable
> - Evaluate the service charge budget and expenditure
> - Investigate repairs and disputes
> - Identify company or trust administration requirements
> - Inform and consult

Should you manage the property yourselves or appoint a managing agent?

There is an alternative to the choice of either managing the property yourselves or appointing a managing agent. This is to manage the property yourselves but to seek assistance when needed, perhaps for accounts or for company secretarial assistance on the administrative aspects of running the company which owns the freehold. Managing the property yourselves does not mean you have to do everything by yourselves.

Some of the factors which could affect your choice are:

○ It can be difficult to manage a large building solely by yourselves, unless your building has committed and able flat owners who have plenty of time on their hands.

○ The flat owners may have had enough of being mismanaged by previous managing agents. There is no reason why flat owners should not manage their own freeholds successfully, despite what the occasional managing agent will advise. After all, people manage their own businesses without managing agents.

○ Employing a managing agent distances you from some of the immediate headaches. You can avoid those difficult moments with your neighbour and, being blunt, you can

TIP

Managing the property yourselves takes commitment, time and ability. If these are lacking employ a managing agent.

blame the managing agent instead of one of your neighbours if things go wrong.

○ Regardless of whether you manage the property yourselves or employ a managing agent, you probably will need advice on running the company which owns the freehold. Who will you ask? Your company's auditors might be the answer.

Managing the property yourselves

The example below illustrates some of the steps involved if you decide to manage the property yourselves.

EXAMPLE

Managing 204 Ramillies Road Limited

Before the initial notice is served, the five flat owners at 204 Ramillies Road ask their solicitor to form 204 Ramillies Road Ltd.

Two flat owners are appointed directors, Mrs Stephens being the director responsible for the service charge and rent accounting, with Mr Ripley being the director responsible for the service charge budget, maintenance and insurance. A local firm of accountants is appointed as the company's auditors. Another flat owner, Mrs Ramsden, is appointed company secretary with additional responsibility for keeping everyone informed about management matters. Mr Hanwell, encountered earlier on in this chapter, offers to help out generally but always seems to be away. Mrs Ramsden circulates a note to the five flat owners, and the one tenant who rents, confirming what has happened and advising who will be responsible for what.

Their solicitor prepares a purchase report setting out the landlord's management responsibilities and the tenants' obligations. The report points out that the tenant who rents is not liable for any service charges and that the company will have to mend the tenant's central heating system which keeps on breaking down. The solicitor also prepares a checklist of Mrs Ramsden's company secretarial duties.

Mrs Stephens sets up the systems for rent and service charge accounting before the freehold is purchased and has a word with the Inland Revenue about tax on the company's income from the rented flat.

Mr Ripley reviews the service charge budget and expenditure. He concludes they will need to increase the service charges to pay for the leaking roof which Mr Hanwell in the top floor flat keeps complaining about. Mrs Ramsden

TIP

Contact an Inspector at your local Inland Revenue Office, or your local Customs & Excise for free advice on tax and VAT.

becomes increasingly concerned about how to interpret the company memorandum and articles. It is decided, to Mrs Ramsden's relief, to seek advice from the company's auditors about company secretarial matters.

Four of the five flat owners meet immediately after the freehold is purchased to review the service charge budget and outstanding repairs. They decide to patch the roof now but to overhaul it next year. Mrs Ramsden tells Mr Hariwell what has been decided but he replies that the roof should be mended immediately.

TIP

It is more effective to pay for company secretarial services than to employ a solicitor to sort out the problems afterwards.

Employing a managing agent

If you decide to appoint a managing agent, you may find it helpful to produce a short note on the responsibilities you want them to take on.

This note could form the starting point for interviews. You could send a copy of the note to prospective managing agents and ask them to come to an interview prepared to make a presentation about their experience, views on managing your property, and proposed fees. You can finalise the note describing their responsibilities when you have decided who to appoint. Do not overlook who will be responsible on the freeholder's side for instructing and liaising with the managing agent.

It is always worth spending a little extra time to make sure the terms of appointment are clear and comprehensive. Apart from the description of responsibilities, the terms of appointment should cover:

○ Progress reports on service charge or other arrears
○ Responsibility for service charge budgets and expenditure
○ The managing agent's level of authority to order repairs or services
○ How money is to be held on your behalf and who has the interest
○ Fees and expenses
○ Duration of appointment and notice period for termination
○ Liaison and meetings with the freeholder.

Managing the property check
• Managing it yourselves is possible but it requires commitment, time and ability. You can buy in specialist services
• Larger, complex properties probably require a managing agent
• Establish detailed terms of appointment for any managing agent

Ordering repairs and services

Much of the cost of managing the building will be spent on repairs, maintenance and services. Some basic points in ordering these are:

○ Assess the type of service or works required. For instance, is it really rising damp or is the dampness caused by a leaking pipe?

○ Describe the works or service precisely, with a plan and specification if appropriate.

○ Draw up conditions of engagement dealing with hours of work, start and completion dates, insurance, method of payment, noise control and rubbish removal.

○ Obtain quotations on a common basis from reputable contractors. You can find out who is reputable by taking up references. Uninsured contractors should be avoided so ask for a copy of their insurance policy.

○ Consult with the tenants and others as required by law and obtain any consents which may be required.

○ Analyse the quotations and make the appointment on behalf of the freeholder.

○ Supervise both the quality of repairs or service and compliance with the conditions of engagement.

○ Pay the contractor in accordance with the contract, provided the work or service is reasonable.

○ Keep copies of the contract documents, invoices and payment records.

When repairs or services are needed and you are unsure about the cause of the problem, you could take advice from a surveyor. The same applies if you are getting out of your depth in ordering the repairs or services. The crux of the matter is to obtain a cost-effective solution, even if the short-term costs are increased by seeking professional advice on the best long-term solution.

TIP

Prevent your builder from deafening you, by specifying in advance when noisy equipment, including radios, can and cannot be used.

Management audits and the codes of practice introduced by the Act are relevant for flat owners who have collectively enfranchised and for those who have extended their leases.

Management audits

The purpose of a management audit is to see if the landlord is managing the building in an efficient and effective manner and to identify whether the service charge payments are being used efficiently and effectively.

Flat owners have sometimes suspected, without being able to prove it, that their building was not being managed efficiently and effectively. The appointment of an auditor enables you to find this out. The auditor has the power to inspect accounts and receipts and to request other documents relating to the service charge.

Who is eligible to request the audit?
There are two conditions:
- In order to qualify a tenant must have a long lease, pay a service charge and not be a business tenant. It is possible for only one tenant in the premises to be eligible.
- All the tenants must have leases from the same landlord if more than one tenant in the premises qualifies.

What is the procedure?
The right to an audit can be claimed by one or both tenants if there are two dwellings. Where there are three or more dwellings, the right can only be exercised if two thirds or more of the tenants who qualify demand it. The tenant, or tenants, then appoint their auditor, who gives the landlord a notice specifying the documents required for inspection. The auditor carries out the inspection and reports back.

Comments
- The auditor can be a qualified accountant, or a Fellow or Associate of the Royal Institution of Chartered Surveyors or the Incorporated Society of Valuers and Auctioneers.
- The conditions for eligibility and the procedures are quite elaborate. Discuss them with your auditor.
- The landlord cannot charge for allowing the auditor to inspect but can charge the service charge account with the cost of making copies of documents.

TAKE CARE !

A management audit could take place in a building which had been collectively enfranchised. Consultation with all the flat owners and tenants is the best way to avoid it.

Codes of practice

The Act gives the Government the power to approve codes of practice concerning the management of residential property. The areas to be covered in the codes will include service charges, the resolution of disputes and competitive tendering. Failure to comply with an approved code of practice will not be an offence but a court or tribunal can admit the code as evidence and can take it into account in its judgement.

If you are managing residential property directly, or through a managing agent, you could find these codes useful. Contact the Royal Institution of Chartered Surveyors for information on their availability. See page v for their address.

Glossary

In the interests of accuracy, this book has used a number of legal and technical terms. These are explained below.

Collective ownership
The joint ownership of property, as in the collective ownership of the freehold through a limited company or trust.

Flat owner
Anyone who owns, as opposed to rents, a flat.

Freeholder
The owner of a freehold interest in a property.

Ground rent
The rent which owners of leasehold flats pay their landlord.

Initial notice
The notice which is given to claim the right to collective enfranchisement.

Interest
A property ownership, as in freehold or leasehold interest.

Landlord
The person on whom you serve the tenant's notice. The landlord may or may not be your freeholder but is responsible for all the subsequent negotiations.

Leaseback
An arrangement where an owner sells the property and then leases it back. Freeholders sometimes do this to raise capital.

Leaseholder
The owner of a leasehold interest in property.

Leasehold enfranchisement
The term used in this book to refer to collective enfranchisement and lease extensions. There are separate rights of leasehold enfranchisement for houses.

Leasehold valuation tribunal
A tribunal which can determine disputes over the terms, including the price, for collective enfranchisement and lease extensions.

Long lease
The term used to refer principally, but not exclusively, to a lease which was granted for twenty-one years or more.

Low rent
A type of ground rent. You must have a low rent to qualify for the rights in the Act.

Marriage value
The additional value which is created when the leasehold and freehold interests in a property are brought together.

Nominee purchaser
The person(s), company or trust responsible in collective enfranchisement for negotiating and acquiring the freehold and other interests.

Participating tenants
The flat owners who claim the right to collective enfranchisement.

Peppercorn rent
A peppercorn rent means that no rent is due. A more exotic alternative found in some leases is to require an annual payment of twelve white roses.

Premises
The building or part of a building where your flat is situated.

Premium
A capital payment. Premiums are often paid for the grant of new residential leases.

Qualifying tenant
A flat owner who, provided other conditions are met, is eligible for collective enfranchisement or a lease extension.

Reversioner
The person on whom you serve the initial notice. This is usually the freeholder. The reversioner is responsible for all the subsequent negotiations.

Tenant's notice
The notice which you serve to exercise your right to a lease extension.

Index

The word 'check' refers to the checklists in the text